HOLY WAR
ON THE HOME FRONT

HOLY WAR
ON THE HOME FRONT

The Secret Islamic Terror Network
in the United States

HARVEY KUSHNER

WITH BART DAVIS

SENTINEL

SENTINEL
Published by the Penguin Group
Penguin Group (USA) Inc., 375 Hudson Street, New York, New York 10014, U.S.A.
Penguin Group (Canada), 10 Alcorn Avenue, Toronto, Ontario, Canada M4V 3B2 (a division
of Pearson Penguin Canada Inc.) • Penguin Books Ltd, 80 Strand, London WC2R 0RL, En-
gland • Penguin Ireland, 25 St. Stephen's Green, Dublin 2, Ireland (a division of Penguin
Books Ltd) • Penguin Books Australia Ltd, 250 Camberwell Road, Camberwell, Victoria 3124,
Australia (a division of Pearson Australia Group Pty Ltd) • Penguin Books India Pvt Ltd, 11
Community Centre, Panchsheel Park, New Delhi – 110 017, India • Penguin Group (NZ), Cnr
Airborne and Rosedale Roads, Albany, Auckland 1310, New Zealand (a division of Pearson
New Zealand Ltd) • Penguin Books (South Africa) (Pty) Ltd, 24 Sturdee Avenue, Rosebank,
Johannesburg 2196, South Africa

Penguin Books Ltd, Registered Offices:
80 Strand, London WC2R 0RL, England

First published in 2004 by Sentinel,
a member of Penguin Group (USA) Inc.

10 9 8 7 6 5 4 3 2 1

LIBRARY OF CONGRESS CATALOGING-IN-PUBLICATION DATA
Kushner, Harvey W.
    Holy war on the home front : the secret Islamic terror net-
work in the United States / Harvey Kushner with Bart Davis.
    p. cm.
    Includes index.
    ISBN 1-59523-002-5
    1. Terrorism—United States.   2. Terrorists—United
States.   3. Islam and terrorism—United States.   I. Davis,
Bart, 1950–   II. Title.

    HV6432.K86   2004
    303.6'25'0973—dc22   2004056480

This book is printed on acid-free paper. ∞

Printed in the United States of America

For his insight and inspiration,
this book is gratefully dedicated
to
Robert Gottlieb

ACKNOWLEDGMENTS

Most of the people who contributed to this book must remain nameless. We are confident they know how grateful we are for their support.

Of those who can be named, foremost is Paul Fedorko, of the Trident Media Group, whose personal dedication and professional expertise were of singular importance to the authors of this book. His equanimity in the face of danger and conflict will remain the standard by which all agents should be judged.

Bernadette Malone's editorial direction and literary advice kept us on course, from inception to completion.

Our thanks to Will Weisser for his support; and to Adrian Zackheim, founder and publisher of Sentinel, who made everything possible.

We also thank:

Mr. Karmin Iasso and British Airways for making our journeys so comfortable.

NL, whose insight and artistry clarified everything for us.

PM, RM, FZ, IA, and SM for valuable suggestions and assistance.

Our special guardian angel, Stuart J. Kobak.

Our deepest appreciation to our families for accepting our absences and for their loving support from beginning to end.

CONTENTS

Introduction: The Fifth Column   xiii

1: Universities   1

2: Charities   21

3: The Prison System   35

4: Mosques   55

5: The Drug Connection   75

6: Counterfeiting Rings   95

7: Media   109

8: Profiling   121

9: Government Agencies   137

Conclusion: Final Thoughts and Suggestions   157

Appendix: Documents   167

Notes   207

Index   219

THE FIFTH COLUMN

Near the end of the Spanish Civil War, General Emilio Mola's army was advancing on Madrid when someone asked him which of his four columns would capture the city. "The fifth column," he replied, meaning the rebel's militant supporters inside the capital whose efforts had already undermined it from within.

On April 28, 1999, a Lebanese man, "KM," entered the United States legally on a nonimmigrant visa that was valid for two years. He found work in New York City on the loading dock of a clothing manufacturer's warehouse, earning about $400 a week in cash. Twenty months later, in December of 2000, KM was stopped by U.S. Customs officials at JFK Airport trying to board a flight back to Lebanon with more than $75,000 in cash, checks, and money orders concealed in his luggage. He was arrested and charged with failing to file a Currency Transaction Report.

KM told the investigating officers that the money had been

given to him by a group of friends to bring to their families back home. Soon after, a dozen "friends" living in Brooklyn, Queens, the Bronx, and Long Island signed sworn affidavits that the money was theirs, in amounts ranging from $1,000 to almost $15,000.

Affidavits notwithstanding, an Equifax credit report done by investigators revealed that KM actually had over a dozen active credit lines totaling more than $20,000, and had opened under a different spelling of his name an additional sixteen credit lines together worth almost $40,000. Investigators also found that KM had been working here since 1992, long before the date of entry on his current visa, but had never filed a U.S. tax return. Further, a subsequent search of his apartment uncovered two Lebanese passports with different passport numbers, which KM had used to enter the United States, and bank checks belonging to "AC," a Middle Eastern man who had also used Lebanese passports with different numbers to enter the country on two occasions.

Investigators at AC's residence found KM's name on the mailbox of one of the apartments at that address—the same address listed in documents with the United States Citizenship and Immigration Services (USCIS, formerly the INS) as home to KM's relative "AM," who confidential sources identified as a member of Amal, the radical Lebanese Shiite militia whose splinter group Hezbollah carried out the 1983 bombings of the U.S. embassy and Marine barracks in Beirut.

AM had been arrested and convicted for grand larceny in

1994, charged with making $10,000 in fraudulent purchases from retail stores. He was sentenced in 1995 to just five years' probation, from which he received an early discharge in 1998. Why wasn't AM deported? Incredibly, he obtained U.S. citizenship while his case was pending. A 2002 confidential memo from the U.S. Probation Department (see the appendix) notes: "It is unknown if AM reported this pending arrest to INS."

Profiling KM and AM: both had opened numerous lines of credit and kept several checking accounts with zero balances and minimal deposits. Both reported meager earnings. Both had been "identified by U.S. intelligence sources as linked to extremist groups." In addition, a relative of KM and AM who lived in their building was observed going over documents and checks with a woman in a parked car and later meeting her for less than five minutes at a Middle Eastern restaurant "where an exchange of documents was suspected." The confidential memo concluded the lifestyle of both AM and KM "is consistent with extremist groups."

So what happened to them?

AM is on probation after serving time for conspiracy to launder the proceeds of narcotics trafficking, which he said he did to get money for tickets to Lebanon to visit his family. A federal judge sentenced him to twenty-one months in prison and a $100 fine.

He moved to Long Island.

For KM's failure to file a currency report, he was put on probation. He then filed for permanent residence based on marriage to his wife, from whom he is separated. One month after 9/11, the INS issued him an Employment Authorization Card.

He now lives and works in New York City.

Both are examples of Militant Islam's secret terror network in the United States.

If you thought 9/11 changed things, think again.

For all the time and money we've spent in the past three years on "security," Americans are no safer. Government agencies are still sloppy, negligent, or worse. For years, federal judges have been probating illegal aliens who are "known or suspected terrorists" back onto our streets. But federal probation officers can't report suspicions of terrorist activity from the felons they supervise because there's no one to report it to. At the same time, a drug worth billions of dollars a year is being smuggled into this country by a Middle Eastern–African–British network, but no one is investigating it—or its links to terrorism. The USCIS Asylum Offices get applications from Middle Easterners who testify to involvement with terrorism, but they can't reject them because the FBI won't return their phone calls.

Don't believe it? Sorry, the following quotes from a decade of documents (see the appendix) say it's true:

From the Chief Deputy U.S. Probation Officer of the Eastern District of New York:

"Additionally, our officers occasionally supervise both known or suspected terrorists who are on parole or probation."

From an official of a USCIS Asylum Office:

"Many of our applicants testify to having committed terrorist acts. Sometimes we have reason to believe they committed such acts even when they do not so testify."

From a 2002 Drug Enforcement Administration intelligence brief:

Individuals of East African and Middle Eastern descent are most often responsible for the import, distribution, and use of this drug. Customs seizures have risen to over seventy tons in 2002, with 2003 total sales of over $1.5 billion.

From a document from the Security Battalion
of the U.S. Marine Corps in Quantico, Virginia:

"I have found that there is a lack of up to date information in the Marine Corps regarding terrorism, which has forced me to go to outside sources to perform my duties."

I have been a terrorism analyst for more than thirty years and have advised numerous government and law-enforcement agencies, including the Federal Bureau of Investigation, the Federal Aviation Administration, the Immigration and Naturalization Service, and the U.S. Customs Service. I have also been a special consultant to the U.S. Probation Department on matters related to criminal investigations, intelligence, and terrorism.

During most of my career I was frustrated by the lack of political will to expose what was happening in America. The government ignored terrorism during the 1990s, giving our enemies time to grow capable of planning and executing the suicide bombings of the Twin Towers and the Pentagon. Long before 9/11, I warned of Militant Islam and the secret Islamic network operating in America. I told them to go after terrorism at a time when stamping it out would have been easy. I reiterated the threat as an expert witness in the U.S. East African embassy bombing trial. I wrote about it in the expert's report for litigation stemming from the 1993 World Trade Center bombing trial. I warned them right up to the morning of 9/11 when America changed forever.

It's important to remember that the people who died in the World Trade Center weren't at war, they were at work. That's where terrorism hits—at our jobs and in our homes. We have a right to know what has to be done to protect us where we raise our families. We have a right to know what's going on right in our own backyards. We don't want to cringe when the electricity goes out, or be afraid every minute we're in the air. We need a fresh voice and a new look at the Holy War being waged against us. We need our elected officials to spell out what they're going to do and to be held accountable for doing it.

The following is from a 1994 article I wrote for the *Journal of the International Association of Law Enforcement Intelligence Analysts:*

It is now time for law enforcement intelligence personnel to re-think their understanding of the Middle Eastern terrorist. It is the duty of every Muslim to practice what is good and to forbid what is evil. All Muslims take this dictate of the Holy Koran as an immutable source of Islamic doctrine. But the new terrorists will use this Koranic dictate to further their own agenda. Count on them to take action; understand that they will.

Ten years after that article appeared, Brian Jenkins, a senior adviser at the RAND Corporation and an authority on political violence, reported to the 9/11 Commission on March 31, 2003:

> In sum, the United States will remain the principal target of al Qaeda. We will confront individual jihadists, small local conspiracies with or without foreign assistance, and potentially large-scale plots involving foreign-based teams.

Despite a decade of warnings, Militant Islam still took us by surprise on 9/11. Three years later, our federal agencies still aren't making the connections and doing what's necessary. Law-enforcement agencies don't understand the nature of Militant Islam. The threat of a terrorist nuclear event inside America is undiminished. The FBI and the CIA joining forces isn't going to happen anytime soon, and getting the Department of Homeland Security up to speed is going to take a lot longer than anyone expected.

How do I know? It is my job to talk about the state of America with those who know it best. In March 2004, I gave a briefing in Washington, D.C., to officers of the Joint Special Operations University, located at Hurlburt Field in Florida. According to an August 30, 2000, Air Force public affairs release, these officers are "at points in their careers where they will assume staff and command roles in the joint arena and will inevitably deal directly with decision makers." I had a late dinner with a group of senior military officers, and one of the highest-ranking army officers attached to DHS told me point-blank: "It won't be until 2006 at best that we'll have a Home-land Security Department even *somewhat* functional."

I spend a lot of time talking to people—not just government and military officials, but street cops and probation officers, too. My sources must feel free to talk to me, so my allegations are sometimes supported by unnamed sources. My guidelines for anonymity are: I will not reveal the identity of sources deal-ing with national security who would face serious conse-quences if exposed, or sources who would face legal jeopardy or loss of livelihood for speaking to me. I will not reveal the identity of military or government officials who, as a matter of policy, do not speak for attribution. My sources must have di-rect knowledge of the information they tell me. Confidential or sensitive documents are redacted to protect law-enforcement officers or ongoing investigations.

It seems so simple to most of us—catch the bad guys, punish the guilty—but elected officials keep coming up with such complicated solutions that even *they* don't seem convinced. Maybe it's a good idea to have another high-profile commission trying to figure out who dropped the ball and let 9/11 happen. God knows the families of the victims have a right to know. But those who claim we have to study history to avoid its mistakes weren't students of General George S. Patton, who said, "No-body ever defended anything successfully, there is only attack and attack and attack some more." President Bush has done well in that area, carrying the fight to Afghanistan and Iraq and thereby eliminating two terrorist states. Yet, for all the time and money and American lives spent since 9/11, is America really safer? The answer is no. We are all just waiting for the other shoe to drop.

There is still time to fix things. America is better at crash programs than any nation in the world. It's as simple as this. If we wake up to the menace of Militant Islam we can defeat it. If we fail to recognize the battle for America is *in* America, we could lose it all.

I chair a department at a university, but I quickly learned when dealing with terrorists that death is not academic. Terrorists kill people. They pull triggers, plant bombs, and blast holes in the New York City skyline.

In my thirty years in counterterrorism, I have never been more worried about my country.

Harvey Kushner
June 2004

HOLY WAR
ON THE HOME FRONT

CHAPTER 1

UNIVERSITIES

The secret Islamic network didn't begin in 2001 when the World Trade Center and the Pentagon were attacked. Nor did it begin in the 1990s when Islamic terrorists *first* attempted to blow up the World Trade Center. It began in the mid-1980s when a tightly knit group of Islamic radicals attended the North Carolina Agricultural and Technical State University in Greensboro. So blatant was the group's Militant Islamic fundamentalism and its hatred of Israel—along with the United States for supporting the Jewish state—that the other students took to calling them "the Mullahs," a title generally denoting Muslim religious leaders.

It would take twenty years for the "Mullahs" to be recognized for who they were and for America to see the structure of the secret Islamic terror network they built. The first "Mullah" was Sami al-Arian, a Ph.D. in computer engineering. The second was al-Arian's future brother-in-law, Mazen al-Najjar, who held a degree in engineering. The third was Khalid "Shaikh" Mohammed, later one of the FBI's most wanted, with a reward of $25 million on his head.

Khalid Mohammed arrived in 1984 to study engineering. Almost twenty years later, he used the knowledge he gained at North Carolina A&T to enable the hijacked jetliners to bring down the World Trade Center towers on 9/11. He had tried before. With his nephew, Ramzi Yousef, Khalid Mohammed planned the first World Trade Center bombing in 1993. They are just two of the many murderers we allowed to be trained at our own universities—on American soil.

However, the "Mullahs" could not have remained hidden in plain sight for so long without friends in high places. Before al-Arian was indicted on charges of helping to finance and run the Palestinian Islamic Jihad, he was present at a conference in Washington also attended by FBI agent Gamal Abdel-Hafiz.

Abdel-Hafiz was part of the FBI investigation into al-Arian's terrorist ties, but in 1998 he refused to secretly record his conversations with al-Arian. It wasn't the first time, although Abdel-Hafiz earned raves for his work on the Lackawanna 6 case, and later became the FBI's legal attaché at the U.S. embassy in Riyadh, Saudi Arabia. In 2002, FBI agent Robert Wright accused Abdel-Hafiz of refusing to let colleagues eavesdrop on a terrorist-financing suspect during a case in Chicago because "a Muslim does not record another Muslim."[1]

An investigation prompted by the accusation brought to light charges by Abdel-Hafiz's ex-wife that in 1989 he faked a burglary and police report to bilk his insurance company—and Abdel-Hafiz failed the FBI polygraph test when he denied it. In 2002, an FBI auditing team sent to investigate the FBI office in Riyadh ended up shredding thousands of documents—including dozens of letters from Saudi security officials containing information about terrorist suspects. At the time, Abdel-Hafiz and his supervisor Wilfred Rattigan, a convert to Islam, were in Mecca for the hajj.

Abdel-Hafiz was fired in March 2003. But one year later, in what *Newsweek* called a "rare decision by the Disciplinary Review Board," the FBI reversed its own Office of Professional Responsibility and reinstated Abdel-Hafiz.[2] *Newsweek* reported the FBI's letter reinstating Abdel-Hafiz called his ex-wife's claims "uncorroborated" and "the failed polygraph examination, considering your past history with that test, were not enough to substantiate her allegations against you."[3]

Today al-Arian awaits trial on charges of terrorism that include funding Hamas through a secret network of front groups and fund-raising arms. Al-Arian has denied the charges. Al-Najjar was arrested in 1997 and deported in 2003. Khalid "Shaikh" Mohammed—linked to the bombing of the USS *Cole*, the murder of journalist Daniel Pearl, and the 9/11 attacks—was finally arrested in Pakistan in March 2003. But how much damage to America did they all do over twenty years? How many agents did they put into place? How much of the secret terror network was overlooked because editors frightened by political correctness told reporters not to investigate people like al-

Arian—which is just what Mike Fechter of the *Tampa Tribune,* whose brilliant investigative reporting was a major cause of al-Arian's downfall, told me happened to him.

America must not be lulled into complacency by thinking some arrests solve our problems. Liberals who let the "Mullahs" use the Bill of Rights as a shield created a terrible legacy. The "Mullahs" came to North Carolina A&T in their midtwenties. How many terrorists were they able to recruit and train in the decades since? These new generations bide their time. They wait. When called upon, they will strike.

Irish writer Bernard MacLaverty described the Troubles in Ireland as the "elephant in the living room." The Islamic Holy War in America is *our* "elephant in the living room." In April 2004, National Security Advisor Condoleezza Rice advised the 9/11 Commission, "We must stay on the offense, to find and defeat the terrorists wherever they live, hide, and plot around the world. If we learned anything after September 11, 2001, it is that we cannot wait while dangers gather."

The founding members of the secret Islamic terror network executed a long-range plan: raise money to fund terrorist activities; support Arab and Muslim demonstrations against our government's foreign policy and its support for Israel; infiltrate our political, economic, and military system to conduct espionage and to buy influence; and use our universities to set up fronts for terrorist organizations, because our academia's commitment to Free Speech and tolerance of diversity will protect them.

Part of the FBI indictment of Sami al-Arian, "Section E., Overt Acts," reads:

(185) On or about November 20, 1995, in Tampa, Florida, SAMI AMIN AL-ARIAN possessed, at his residence:

(1) A document entitled the "Charter of the Center of Studies, the Intelligence and the Information," which set forth a detailed description of the structure and operation of a hostile intelligence organization in the United States and elsewhere. The document included the organizational structure, duties, responsibilities, espionage methods and targets, counterintelligence and precautionary measures, methods of reporting and a cipher system to make the hostile intelligence organization appear to be *affiliated with a university* [emphasis added].

The "Charter of the Center of Studies" was handwritten in Arabic and dated 1981 (see the appendix). It is a Militant Islamic organizational plan for terrorism, with every cell, division, agent, and objective clearly defined. One expert's opinion regarding the original Arabic is that the document could have originated from the ranks of the Muslim Brotherhood, the originator of all contemporary Militant Islamic movements.

Along with the charter, investigators found a separate sheet of paper with a hand-drawn map of the United States and Canada, more proof that Militant Islam has been building the secret terror network inside North America for decades. The map is divided into four sections:

The Western Region, with dots on the cities of San Francisco, Los Angeles, and Denver.

The Central Region, with dots on Houston, New Orleans, St. Louis, Chicago, Indianapolis, and Detroit.

The Eastern Region, with dots on Boston, New York, Philadelphia, Washington, Raleigh, and Miami.

The Canadian Region, with dots on Toronto and Montreal.

A DEMONSTRATIVE ILLUSTRATION OF THE LOCATION OF THE TEAM OF RESEARCHERS. THE BUREAU OF NORTH AMERICA is written underneath the drawing.

In 1981, few, if any, terrorist groups were in the cities labeled in Arabic on the map (see the appendix). Today there are terrorist groups in *every* city shown on the map, proof of how far the network has spread:

BOSTON
Al Qaeda
Hamas

NEW YORK
Al Qaeda
Al Muhajiroun
Gama'a al-Islamiyya
Hezbollah
Hamas
PLO
Fatah

PHILADELPHIA
Al Qaeda
Al Muhajiroun
Gama'a al-Islamiyya
Hezbollah
Hamas
PLO
Fatah

WASHINGTON, D.C.
Hezbollah
Hamas
Al Qaeda
Palestinian Islamic Jihad

RALEIGH
Hamas
Palestinian Islamic Jihad

MIAMI
Hamas
Palestinian Islamic Jihad
Fatah
PLO

NEW ORLEANS
Hamas

DETROIT
Gama'a al-Islamiyya
Hezbollah
Hamas
PLO
Fatah

INDIANAPOLIS
Hamas

CINCINNATI
Hamas

ST. LOUIS
Abu Nidal Organization

HOUSTON
Al Qaeda
Hamas
Muslim Brotherhood
Palestinian Islamic Jihad

DENVER
Hamas

SAN FRANCISCO
Al Qaeda
Hamas
Abu Sayyaf Group

LOS ANGELES
Hamas
Gama'a al-Islamiyya
Al Qaeda

Americans have been looking at these pieces of the puzzle for years but still won't accept that the pieces are connected. No one wants to sound bigoted against a religious group, and connecting the puzzle pieces creates an uncomfortable picture few want to acknowledge. America's Islamic enemies came here hidden among millions of legitimate immigrants from the Middle East, North Africa, Pakistan, and a host of other countries. This virulent Muslim minority hates everything America stands for and has built a secret network of Islamic organizations and individuals that includes charities, drug dealers, university professors, lawyers, liberal organizations, violent criminals, imams, spies, and traitors. In addition to its terror operations, the secret network maintains a campaign of incendiary hate speech to manipulate entire Muslim communities into isolation, alienation, and the sick eagerness to be used as cannon fodder.

The global spread of Militant Islam has its roots in the radical fundamentalism that fueled the Iranian revolution in 1979. The new religious government in Tehran became a link between terror organizations like Hezbollah and Islamic Jihad. Hezbollah was responsible for blowing up the U.S. Marine barracks in Lebanon and kidnapping Americans, such as Terry Anderson and Beirut CIA Station Chief William Buckley, the latter dying in captivity with nine others.

The Soviet invasion of Afghanistan in 1979 made Militant Islam stronger. The war gave practical training to the Mujahideen fighters in a real theater of operations. With the defeat of the Soviets in 1989, the Mujahideen veterans split into three camps: Some immigrated to the United States and Canada.

Some stayed in Afghanistan with Osama bin Laden to form al Qaeda. Some joined terrorist groups already in existence.

The Mujahideen became a new brand of terrorist—uncompromising 24/7 professional "Jihadists" with ten years' experience fighting, and defeating, a superpower. These same Jihadists are fighting the Holy War on our home front. They are battle-scarred veterans with complete faith that God wants them to destroy America—and God allows no compromise. We can no longer ignore their presence. No matter how politically incorrect it sounds, we have the right to use all resources necessary to catch the terrorists who, in the years after September 11, have forced us to be sniffed, scanned, and searched before boarding our own planes. Thinking *Terrorism* the moment the electricity goes out is a sign we haven't been honest about what we want from those entrusted to protect us, or the lengths to which we want them to go to eliminate the menace.

Americans have to advocate fighting back, but we've been frightened into silence by political correctness and the ghosts of our past. We've ignored what we know about human nature. We refuse to connect the hate speech pouring out of Islamic religious and political leaders, even when terrorist letters claim responsibility for murder with the same words. We ignore anti-American rhetoric from Islamic professors, imams, and Muslim leaders as if sedition were protected speech.

Militant Islam wants to change America. Its rhetoric is protected—and often admired—by campus liberals. It is often spawned by Islamic studies departments and characterized by opposition to American foreign policy and a never-ending effort to make Israel vulnerable by lessening U.S. support. It is almost always spread by Islamic university professors under the banner of their right to inject what they call their "viewpoint" into the public dialogue.

A case in point is the Edward Said Chair of Arab Studies at Columbia University, given to Rashid Khalidi, a University of Chicago historian and a Palestinian activist. It is a $2.1 million endowment paid for in large part by the United Arab Emirates. Despite the huge sums of money involved, Columbia claims that donors of the endowment have no influence over Rashid Khalidi or any other person appointed the position in the future.

Khalidi wrote in "American Anointed":

> And if there is disillusionment, anger, even hatred for the United States in many countries in these regions, it is not necessary to look at Islamic doctrine, at the alleged propensity of Muslims for violence, or at the supposed centrality of the concept of jihad to Islam for the causes. One need look no further than the corrupt and autocratic regimes propped up by the United States, and its disregard for the opinions of Middle Eastern peoples regarding Palestine, sanctions on Iraq, and other issues.[4]

Islamic university professors are often supported by their non-Muslim colleagues who blame America first in world affairs. Columbia University professor of anthropology and Latin American studies Nicholas De Genova said, "U.S. flags are the emblem of the invading war machine in Iraq today. They are the emblem of the occupying power. The only true heroes are those who find ways that help defeat the U.S. military."5 Their attempt to influence public discussion has already been partially successful, establishing a false "moral equivalency" between Militant Islam's use of suicide bombers to blow up children at bus stops and America's use of military force against military targets during a war.

Institutions of higher education occupy a hallowed place in this country. They promote the free exchange of ideas and are rarely subject to government scrutiny. It makes universities the perfect place for Militant Islam to hide. Is generosity the only reason the Bin Laden family gives millions to Harvard, including endowments to Harvard Law School to study legal institutions in Islamic states, and to Harvard Design School to study Islamic architecture? For what reason does Harvard adopt an "innocent until proven guilty" attitude toward Bin Laden family money—considering there is at least a familial link to Osama—but won't allow the ROTC on campus?

The climate at universities is nearly always hospitable to critics of U.S. foeign policy. but rarely to their opponents. Journalists Asaf Romirowsky and Jonathan Calt Harris cite the following examples in their January 28, 2004, article, "The Campus Left: Opposing Free Speech by Force":

• In September 2002, the former prime minister of Israel Benjamin Netanyahu could not speak at Concordia University in Montreal because anti-Israel protestors rioted, "smashing windows and hurling furniture at police, kicking and spitting on people going to the event."

• When Palestinian activist Hanan Ashrawi spoke at the

University of Pennsylvania and the president of the sponsoring Arab Student Society said, "I was very happy with the way the crowd showed her a lot of respect."

• When Daniel Pipes, Harvard Ph.D. and director of the Middle East Forum, tried to speak at York University in Toronto, the administration imposed strict security, including "a 24-hour lockdown on the building beforehand, metal detectors for the audience, identification checks," and dozens of police officers standing by to enforce the warning that hecklers would be forcibly removed. Police had earlier responded to a bomb scare and fire alarm.

• John Esposito, head of Georgetown University's Center for Muslim-Christian Understanding and a former adviser to the Clinton State Department, required no special security when he delivered the keynote address at Stanford University's inauguration of the new Islamic Studies program.

The secret Islamic network was built on media, money, and manpower. One part of it hides in our universities and uses academic freedom to avoid scrutiny as it advances the agenda of its Holy War. It promotes its political view in every form of media, from scholarly publications to TV talk shows. Sami al-Arian's infiltration of the University of South Florida at Tampa contaminated classrooms and conferences. The quasi-academic organizations the secret network developed, such as the Islamic Committee for Palestine (ICP) and the World and Islam Studies Enterprise (WISE), sponsored many conferences to discuss world politics—a subject not part of their founder's area of doctoral training. They were nothing but groups designed to turn students and other participants against America's foreign policy. The plan not only went unnoticed, it was welcomed.

The USF faculty, even Jewish professors upset by al-Arian's pro-Palestinian stance and anti-U.S. policy toward Israel, allowed al-Arian a decade to build his secret network, recruit others, and put his plans into action—shielded by academic freedom.

At a recent conference I attended, a former USF professor who knew Sami al-Arian told me that during al-Arian's stay at USF, many of the faculty sought his friendship. He was a power at the university. The university administration liked al-Arian because he brought international figures to USF, which was, at that time, trying to build up its reputation to get a bigger share of the state's education pie.

In January 1986, al-Arian accepted a tenure-track appointment as assistant professor at the University of South Florida's College of Engineering at Tampa to teach computer science. Within two years of his hiring at USF, he legally incorporated the Islamic Concern Project, an umbrella organization that included the ICP. The ICP supported Palestinian causes, including the responsibility for informing the American public about the 1987 Intifada, the Palestinian uprising against Israel's occupation of the West Bank and Gaza. At a 1990 event commemorating the thousandth day of the Intifada, al-Arian restated in Arabic what he had said earlier in 1988:

"God is one, Mohammed is our Leader, the Koran is our Constitution. Struggling in the cause of God is our way. Victory to Islam,
death to Israel. Revolution, revolution until victory. March, march
toward Jerusalem. There is no deity but God. Mohammed is the
Messenger of God. God is great. Victory to Islam."[6]

In 1991, al-Arian legally incorporated the World and Islamic
Studies Enterprise (WISE), ostensibly a Tampa think tank
devoted to Islamic thought and political theory. Al-Arian was
helped by Basheer Musa Mohammed Nafi, alleged by the U.S.
government in an indictment to be the head of the terror group
Islamic Jihad in Britain. Nafi came to a Tampa meeting that
began negotiations for an agreement between WISE and USF's
Committee for Middle Eastern Studies. Professors at USF-
Tampa told me how they were shocked at the relative ease with
which USF approved of al-Arian's projects. As a rule, universities require significant vetting of the money that flows into the
institution to support a project that has any affiliation with the
university.

Nafi went on to a group based in Herndon, Virginia, the In-
ternational Institute for Islamic Thought (IIIT). While at IIIT,
Nafi reportedly funneled money into al-Arian's WISE project.
Like al-Arian, Nafi held a doctorate in a hard science, biology.
Nafi's résumé puts him studying in Egypt at Cairo University
from 1971 to 1981. That puts Nafi in Egypt at the same time
Fathi Shikaki and Ramadan Abdullah al-Shallah were at Zagazig
University establishing the PIJ.

Last year, U.S. Attorney General John Ashcroft announced

the indictment of Nafi along with seven other men. Aschroft accused Nafi of being the British head of the Palestinian Islamic Jihad. If so, Nafi is responsible for more than one hundred killings, including suicide bombings, car bombings, and drive-by shootings in and around Israel, some of which included American citizens. Questioned last year, Nafi said of his relationship with al-Arian, "Of course I have spoken with Sami al-Arian. He is a friend, a good friend of mine."[7] (Nafi has denied any connection with Islamic Jihad.

In 1995, federal agents descended on WISE headquarters, al-Arian's office at USF, and his home. The affidavit used to obtain the search warrants described WISE and the ICP as fronts for the PIJ.[8] The FBI seized tapes from the late 1980s and the early 1990s in which al-Arian proclaims in Arabic, "Death to Israel" and "Let us damn America."[9]

In 1997, federal agents arrested al-Arian's brother-in-law, Mazen al-Najjar, who worked at WISE and the ICP. He entered the country from Gaza in December 1981 on a student visa. Al-Najjar was al-Arian's close childhood friend and also attended North Carolina Agricultural and Technical State University. Al-Najjar fought a deportation order and was jailed as a security threat.

Al-Najjar spent three and a half years in jail before his release on December 15, 2000. However, in response to an ACLU brief, the court decided the use of such evidence violated al-Najjar's rights, even though al-Najjar's ICP was responsible for helping known terrorists obtain visas to enter the United States.[10] He went free but was arrested by federal agents on November 24,

2001, after the court ordered him deported. His attorneys sued, arguing there wasn't a host country to take him.

While al-Najjar was back in prison fighting deportation, al-Arian was busy fighting his own case with USF and the federal authorities. Al-Arian was a showman and a self-promoter. A professor at USF who knew al-Arian said he thought Sami's real downfall was his desire for publicity, and if he hadn't gone on Fox's *The O'Reilly Factor,* he might still be at USF. However, host Bill O'Reilly, an unrelentingly confrontational interviewer, grilled al-Arian about his relationship with Shallah and remarks he made about "Death to Israel." It was the beginning of the end, but al-Arian tried to limit the damage by appearing on a talk show hosted by a much friendlier and far more liberal Phil Donahue. This exchange was a real highlight, demonstrating how far a liberal can bend over backward: "So, one more time, sir," said interviewer Phil Donahue to Professor Sami al-Arian, "and I know that you're probably getting tired of these same questions—'Death to Israel' did not mean you wanted to kill Jews, do I understand your position?"[11]

On February 21, 2002, federal authorities confirmed an active investigation into the conduct of Professor Al-Arian. On March 20, 2002, federal officers again executed search warrants on al-Arian and WISE and fifteen other Muslim businesses and charities in connection with investigations into terrorist funding.

On August 21, the same day his brother-in-law Mazen al-Najjar was deported, USF lawyers asked a state judge to rule on whether firing al-Arian would violate his First Amendment rights. President Judy Genshaft finally said, "After all I have seen and heard, I believe that Dr. Al-Arian has abused his position at the university and is using academic freedom as a shield to cover improper activities."[12] The USF lawsuit accused al-Arian of having ties to terrorism that "adversely affect the legitimate interests of the university."[13]

The Coalition of Progressive Student Organizations, representing fifteen student groups at USF, published a letter of support in the name of academic Free Speech: "In an unanimous vote on Wednesday, January 9th, the Coalition of Progressive Student Organizations at USF voted to resolve to not support the Board of Trustee's recommendation to terminate Dr. Sami Al-Arian and President Genshaft's decision to effect their decision. This stance of The Coalition was made in alliance with the Muslim Student Association and with the input of members of the Graduate Students United of USF."[14]

The Coalition listed among its members and student organization affiliates the Africana Studies Club, Amnesty International, the Campus Greens, the College Democrats, Cuba Vive, Free the Planet!, the NAACP, NOW@USF, the Student Environmental Association, the Students for International Peace & Justice, the PRIDE Alliance, the Shanachie, the Muslim Student Association, and the Free Thinkers. The letter concluded: ". . . as this university has terminated Dr. Al-Arian for reasons other than those for which he is officially charged, we a collective student voice, deplore the Board of Trustees for committing an injustice against a tenured faculty professor. This scenario would render students to the possibility of wanton discipline. We impress upon the BOT to be mindful of the diploma that we shall always display, bearing the name of University of South Florida, and the reputation it carries with it. [signed] Anthony T. Brooks, Chairman, The Coalition, University of South Florida."[15]

On February 20, 2003, a federal indictment accused al-Arian of being a principal in the Palestinian Islamic Jihad. The professor and seven other co-conspirators were charged with running a criminal enterprise in the United States and conspiring to kill and maim others abroad.

Federal agents arrested University of South Florida Professor Sami al-Arian on February 20, 2003, along with seven others, charged with providing material support to terrorists—after denying terrorist connections for almost twenty years. Shamelessly, al-Arian rallied the faculty under the banner of Free Speech, again claiming he was the victim of persecution and prejudice. In a speech to the faculty, he said, "During my career, I have never brought any politics to the classroom, my department, or the university."[16]

He neglected to mention an astonishingly long list of items, among them an e-mail sent to him by a professor at a Middle Eastern Studies department that offers: "[c]ondolences for the death of the brother. I was terribly saddened at hearing the news."

Based on my analysis, the dead "brother" referred to in the e-mail can only have been Dr. Fathi Shaqaqi, leader of the PIJ terrorist group, killed on October 26, 1995, on the island of

Malta. In a stunning example of how the Islamic terror network functions, Professor Ramadan Abdullah al-Shallah—who had been brought to USF by Sami al-Arian—immediately left Florida and flew to the Middle East to replace Shaqaqi as leader of the Palestinian Islamic Jihad. His leadership included the March 1996 suicide bombing in Tel Aviv that killed twenty civilians and wounded more than seventy-five, including two Americans.

To answer the question of whether al-Arian knew of Shaqaqi's death, here is FBI wiretap evidence cited in his indictment:

UNITED STATES DISTRICT COURT
MIDDLE DISTRICT OF FLORIDA
TAMPA DIVISION

UNITED STATES OF AMERICA
v
SAMI AMIN AL-ARIAN   CASE No. 8:03-CR-77

181) On or about October 30, 1995, in the early morning hours, SAMI AMIN AL-ARIAN received a telephone call from Unindicted Co-Conspirator Two in which Unindicted Co-Conspirator Two asked whether SAMI AMIN AL-ARIAN had heard that Fathi Shiqaqi had been killed. SAMI AMIN AL-ARIAN indicated he had heard and then refused to talk.

Al-Arian also neglected to mention what he wrote when a terrorist attack killed nineteen Israeli soldiers earlier that year: "The link with the brothers in Hamas is very good and making steady progress, and there are serious attempts at unification and permanent coordination. I call upon you to try to extend true support to the jihad effort so that operations such as these can continue."[17]

There continues to be mounting evidence of the longtime presence of the Islamic terrorist network at USF-Tampa. The danger to us is that it's operating at other American universities, too, using the Bill of Rights as a shield. That shield is not impenetrable, however. A lying professor or a lying cleric is just that—a liar. The constitutional protections of Freedom of Speech and Freedom of Religion do not prevent prosecuting *anyone* who uses public speech or religious ministry to commit a crime.

CHAPTER 2

CHARITIES

There appears to be significant evidence that the secret Islamic terror network had an invaluable asset in Sami al-Arian. But it still needed money to operate. The job of getting the cash belonged to Musa Mohammed Abu Marzook.

Abu Marzook was born in a Gaza refugee camp in 1951. He studied at the Helwan College of Engineering and Technology in Cairo and came to the United States in the early 1980s. He earned a master's degree in industrial engineering at Colorado State University and a Ph.D. in engineering from Columbia State University in 1991.

Abu Marzook joined Hamas in 1992 and quickly became deputy chief of its political bureau in the United States. He moved to a suburb outside of Washington, D.C., with his wife and family. Four of Abu Marzook's children were born in this country.

Abu Marzook consistently denied he had any connection to the military wing of Hamas. He compared his role to that of Gerry Adams, president of Sinn Féin, the political party long associated with the Irish Republican Army. Abu Marzook claimed his job was to just raise funds for "political action initiatives" in the United States. To that end, he built an international financial and political support network that raised hundreds of millions of dollars over the years.

Abu Marzook spread money around—a lot of money. He was welcomed at the Clinton White House. He had top-level briefings there. The Democrats overlooked Abu Marzook's founding of the anti-American Islamic Association for Palestine (IAP), headquartered in Richardson, Texas. They ignored IAP inviting Hamas terrorists and radical clerics as keynote speakers at their annual gatherings. At the IAP's 1989 Kansas City convention, the keynote address was delivered by a terrorist wearing a veil to conceal his identity who recounted one of his own personal acts of sabotage—the blowing up of a bus in Israel that resulted in the death of sixteen people.[1]

A few people did see through Abu Marzook. Former FBI Counterterrorism Chief Oliver Revell told the *Washington Post,* "IAP is a Hamas front. . . . It's controlled by Hamas, it brings Hamas leaders to the U.S., it does propaganda for Hamas."[2] No one in the Clinton administration paid attention. Neither did anyone bother to look at tax records showing that in 1993 Abu Marzook donated a cash payment of $210,000 to the IAP-linked Holy Land Foundation for Relief and Development (HLF).[3]

At the International Policy Institute for Counter-Terrorism

in Herzliya, Israel, in early 2004, I spoke with famed terrorism expert Dr. Boaz Ganor and Colonel Jonathan Fighel (ret.), whom Ganor described as his "right hand." Colonel Fighel told me of an incident in 1992 when he was military governor of the town of Jenin in Israel. Fighel said a 1992 raid on a Hamas "center" in Jenin uncovered a cache of Holy Land Foundation documents identifying the organization as an arm of al Qaeda, as well as connecting "people" in England to "people" in Chicago. There were also checks drawn on American banks made out to the Holy Land Foundation. Such links to the United States were rare at that time. It was important enough to be classified and given to (now) Brigadier General Dani Arditi, director of the Counter-Terrorism Bureau of Security Council, Israel, and Udi Levi of the Counter-Terrorism Branch, who informed the FBI of the find.

However, some years later, when Fighel had cause to mention the checks and documents to the FBI, the agent he spoke with could not recall any mention of them. If evidence linking the HLF to al Qaeda was available as early as 1992, why did it take until 2001 for the FBI to charge Abu Marzook with using the HLF as a money conduit to Hamas, freeze its assets, and have U.S. Treasury Secretary Paul O'Neill tell the press, "The Holy Land Foundation masquerades as a charity, while its primary purpose is to fund Hamas"?[4]

It is an indictment of the Clinton administration. President Clinton ignored IRS records showing that over 10 percent of HLF funds in 1992 came from Abu Marzook. The intelligence community was left to limp along without the updating it needed after the Cold War. During the president's entire tenure in office, the Holy Land Foundation continued to fund Hamas. Could 9/11 have been prevented if an investigation had aggressively pursued the evidence of terrorist activity a decade earlier?

The Islamic secret network's complicated web of multialphabet acronym organizations and interlocking directorates helps conceal their activities. One of the two officials of the Islamic Association for Palestine is also a founding board member of the Council on American-Islamic Relations (CAIR) and publicly supports Hamas terrorist activities. Ghassan Elashi, a founding board member of the Texas chapter of CAIR, was at one time also the chairman of the same Holy Land Foundation (HLF) that the government shut down for funding Hamas.[5]

The Council on American-Islamic Relations bills itself as the voice of moderate Muslims. It had meetings with high-level officials in the Clinton administration. CAIR and other national Islamic organizations used those high-level interactions to meet and influence government officials. There can be no security in government if the gatekeepers leave the gates open to supporters of terrorist organizations like Hamas.

These events finally prompted American authorities to take a longer look at Abu Marzook and his activities. Returning from a trip abroad, Abu Marzook was denied entrance into America and detained as a Hamas operative. Muslims for a Better America, a subgroup of the American Muslim Council, joined with CAIR and the IAP to protest Abu Marzook's detention. A press statement from the Marzook Legal Fund expressed "the concern that our judicial system has been kidnapped by Israeli interests."[6]

During Abu Marzook's detention, his chief advocate on television and in the news was Abdurahman Muhammad Alamoudi. Alamoudi appeared in interviews and current events programs, once opposite me on a Fox News Channel panel debate. Alamoudi claimed I was labeling Abu Marzook a terrorist just because he was a Muslim and insisted Abu Marzook was not part of any terrorist group.

Alamoudi's role trumpeting Abu Marzook's unjust accusation kept him in personal contact with Abu Marzook even during the two years Abu Marzook was incarcerated at the Manhattan Correctional Center in New York City. Hamas leaders had to keep in touch with him through his lawyer, Stanley Cohen.[7]

The Israelis took action on two fronts. They informed the FBI that hundreds of thousands of dollars were transferred from Abu Marzook's account into a bank account of Chicago auto dealer Muhammad Salah. Salah was subsequently arrested in Israel for distributing money to the military wing of Hamas.[8] The Israelis then called for Abu Marzook's extradition, citing his tie to at least ten violent Hamas attacks between 1990 and 1994. The courts dragged on so long, however, that by the time a U.S. district court judge ruled that Abu Marzook could be extradited, Israel's new prime minister, Benjamin Netanyahu, dropped the request, fearing the possibility of an outbreak of Hamas violence in retaliation. After secret meetings between then-FBI director Louis Freeh and the late King Hussein, Abu Marzook was finally sent to Jordan.

He left Jordan in response to a crackdown on Hamas. Traveling on a Yemeni passport, he slipped into Syria. He resides in Damascus, where he can help direct Hamas international activities without interference.[9]

Abu Marzook's absence could have left a gaping hole in the terror network's leadership, coming at a moment when it now had the money and media presence to make the leap to political power. But Abdurahman Muhammad Alamoudi, Abu Marzook's former chief advocate on American television and in newspapers, filled the gap. The international organization Musa Mohammed Abu Marzook had built to fund Militant Islam and the Jihadists' Holy War in America went to Alamoudi.

Alamoudi used the house that Abu Marzook had built to make himself prominent in national Muslim affairs. He became a familiar face in Washington. He met with President Clinton and made six trips to Muslim nations as a goodwill ambassador for the State Department. In 2002, FBI Director Robert Mueller even spoke at an event of the American Muslim Council (AMC), an organization founded by Alamoudi.[10] Despite his public support for Hamas and Hezbollah,[11] Alamoudi was invited to meet with candidate George W. Bush in Austin, Texas, in 2000, and was invited to join President Bush at prayer services for the victims of the 9/11 terror attacks. Alamoudi also attended political briefings in the White House in the summer of 2001.

The American Muslim Council was one of the national Islamic organizations Alamoudi created as his star rose within the Clinton and Bush administrations. FBI Director Mueller even spoke at an AMC national convention in June 2002— against the advice of national security groups for what they said amounted to "political cover" for the AMC. An FBI spokesman countered by claiming the AMC was one of the most "mainstream" Muslim groups in the country.

Alamoudi was delighted. He said in a June 19, 2002, statement posted on IslamOnline.com, "I am very pleased that at least there are some people who are in the administration who call people by their names—yes, the American Muslim Council, whether [critics like it] or not, we are a mainstream organization, and we are the senior mainstream [Muslim] political organization in Washington."

His way of hiding was to be prominent, so that no one could accuse him of anything, much less investigate him. Alamoudi's invitations to the White House and meetings with President Clinton gave him a lot of influence. He used it to make friends, silence critics, and hide influence-buying into Washington's most prominent circles.

Alamoudi's downfall began on Wednesday, August 13, 2003, in London. Alamoudi was a guest at the Hotel Metropole. As founder of the American Muslim Council and now president of the American Muslim Foundation, Alamoudi traveled frequently. He liked the Metropole. It catered to an international clientele, and its central location made it a convenient place to receive visitors.

The only visitor Alamoudi received on the morning of the thirteenth was a Libyan who brought a small Samsonite-type briefcase filled with cash—$340,000 packed in thirty-four bundles of sequentially numbered one-hundred-dollar bills.[12]

Alamoudi tried to leave London for Damascus three days later, but alert Customs officers at Heathrow Airport found the money in his suitcase. They detained Alamoudi while agents of Scotland Yard's Special Branch were brought in to investigate. They found that Alamoudi had been traveling for almost a month and had visited seven countries. He used a U.S. passport to enter England and Saudi Arabia; a Yemeni passport to enter Lebanon, Syria, Yemen, Egypt, and Libya. He had a third passport, from Libya, in his papers.

Alamoudi told the agents that the money was just an innocent donation to the American Muslim Foundation from a sympathetic group in Libya. He insisted the money was to be deposited in a Saudi bank and would have been transferred back to America as it was needed. He told the investigators it was the only such donation he had received from the Libyan organization.

"Financing the work," he went on, "is a constant struggle." Actually, finding financing wasn't quite the struggle Alamoudi made it out to be. The money brought to his hotel did indeed come from Libya, but it was not the first time such a cash drop had occurred, as the investigators learned when they began to reconstruct the chain of events.

As far back as 1997, Alamoudi had met with Libya's ambassador to the United Nations, Abuzed O. Dorda, and discussed Libya's American assets that had been frozen by the U.S. government in response to the downing of Pan Am Flight 103.

Dorda offered Alamoudi a percentage of any funds he could get released. Alamoudi agreed to use his contacts and actually had several meetings with White House officials about the matter. Meanwhile, Dorda was arranging to help Alamoudi with his "struggle" for funding. He sent Alamoudi to meet the president of the Tripoli-based World Islamic Call Society, Mohamed Ahmed al-Sharif, with the understanding that al-Sharif would be of assistance.

Alamoudi met al-Sharif in Tripoli on at least ten occasions. When asked by one of the British agents at Heathrow why he, a naturalized American citizen, would do business with a country responsible for terrorist attacks on Americans, Alamoudi responded that he wanted to "bridge the gulf" between his adopted country and the Islamic state.[13]

The Libyan World Islamic Call Society was no let's-bridge-the-gulf-with-America group. It was a quasi-governmental agency created by Muammar Qaddafi to oversee the state-approved religion and export Libya's radical Islamic ideology abroad.[14] The money Alamoudi received at the Metropole was indeed from al-Sharif, but the "innocent cash donation" had a sinister purpose. Nor was it the only time Alamoudi had received such large sums from Libya.

Alamoudi also had all the skill of a magician in making cash from Libya and Syria disappear and reappear in the United States. When he went to London that August and checked into the Metropole, he was consolidating a critical phase of his infiltration of America. He'd used $2.5 million in no-interest loans from the Islamic Development Bank and the Saudi Economic Development Company to buy a building for "the permanent quarters of the American Muslim Council, the American Muslim Foundation, and the Hajj Foundation."[15] The money he received from the World Islamic Call Society was in fact to repay the loans.

Alamoudi's plan was to use the building as headquarters for a far more deeply entrenched and effective Islamic network. As will be seen, he had laid all the groundwork. With the Libyan money, success was almost assured. He could expand operations and be more influential in American politics. His cash would sustain it all. Only one thing remained.

No violence-oriented terrorist group including Hamas and al Qaeda could plan effective, or even viable operations, without information. Someone has to know about airport security. Someone has to know how to rent cars, get credit cards, and disperse cash. Someone has to know where to buy guns; someone else has to know where to store them. Only someone living here, someone who knows us—knows what will hurt us most.

When British authorities returned Alamoudi to the United States, he was arrested at Dulles Airport on the basis of the criminal complaint filed in the U.S. District Court in Alexandria, Virginia, by Immigration and Customs Enforcement Special Agent Brett Gentrup, on September 29, 2003. The federal charges included prohibiting financial transactions with the Libyan government; prohibiting transactions with Libya; money laundering; money structuring; misuse of passport; unlawful procurement of naturalization; and failure to report foreign bank accounts.[16] Prosecutors "also accused him [Alamoudi] of having financial ties to al Qaeda and other terrorist groups."[17]

The American Muslim Armed Forces and Veterans Affairs Council is one of three Pentagon-approved groups that endorses Muslim military chaplains. The other is the Islamic Society of North America (ISNA) at the Graduate School of Islamic and Social Sciences (GSISS) in Leesburg, Virginia. Since Alamoudi's arrest, the Pentagon has ordered a review of how it recruits military chaplains, particularly Muslim clerics. Closing the barn door well after the cow has gone, the Pentagon stressed it will look at those "endorsed by U.S. Muslim groups with ties to radical Islam."[18]

Arizona Republican Senator Jon Kyl said on October 14, 2003, "It is remarkable that people who have known connections to terrorism are the only people to approve these chaplains."[19] It is also remarkable that after telling a rally outside the White House in 2000, "We are all supporters of Hamas. Allahu Akbar! . . . I am also a supporter of Hizballah,"[20] and defending Hamas during a visit to the Clinton White House, Alamoudi donated $50,000 to Hillary Clinton's Senate campaign during a June 2000 fund-raiser in Boston. The Clinton campaign listed the donation as having come from the American Muslim Council, although that later was described as a typographical error.

The Islamic network's public relations campaign seeks moral equivalency by spreading terrorist disinformation rather than political dissent. Here are some examples:

After President George W. Bush closed the Holy Land Foundation, which had raised $13 million for Hamas in its last year of operation, AMC condemned it as "particularly disturbing . . . unjust and counterproductive."[21] The Council on American-Islamic Relations issued a statement, too, expressing "deep concern" over Alamoudi's arrest. CAIR Board Chairman Omar Ahmad stated, "We are very concerned that the government would bring charges after investigating an individual for many years without offering any evidence of criminal activity." Ahmad further said that Alamoudi's arrest "could leave the impression that [it] is based on political considerations, not legitimate national security concerns."[22]

Facts must replace lies. Our government and our military have been penetrated by Militant Islamic spies. Alamoudi's acceptance by senior American officials let him establish the American Muslim Council and the American Muslim Foundation. His ability to consult with officials at the Pentagon for over a decade enabled him to establish the American Muslim Armed Forces and Veterans Affairs Council to train and certify Islamic chaplains for the U.S. Army Corps of Chaplains.

The following excerpt is from a January 28, 2002, article:

Muslim chaplain sent to Guantanamo

WASHINGTON (RNS)—The U.S. military has decided to send a Muslim chaplain to Guantanamo Bay, Cuba, to help meet the religious needs of Taliban detainees. The military base at that location has an on-site Catholic chaplain but no Muslim chaplains, reported the Washington Post. Air Force Maj. Eddy Villavivencio, spokesman for the U.S. Southern Command, said a Muslim chaplain in the U.S. Navy arrived at the site during the week of Jan. 20. "There are not that many Muslim chaplains in the U.S. military," he said. "One is being provided should any of the detainees wish access to a minister of that faith." The action follows stated concerns by rights groups about U.S. treatment of the al-Qaida and Taliban detainees.[23]

Former high-level CIA sources have told me that they believe Alamoudi's American Muslim Armed Forces and Veterans Affairs Council was an intelligence operation from the start, used to penetrate the American military. The operation inserted Muslim agents into the prison at Guantanamo to gain information from Arab detainees. No charges have been filed against this organization.

What would Hamas or even al Qaeda want from Guantanamo or the prisoners there? What information wouldn't be too old to matter, however high ranking the inmate? No terrorist group could attack the base to break anybody out, nor would they need to—Hamas and al Qaeda will continue to function if the detainees are held forever.

According to one of my sources in the CIA, the penetration of the prison at Guantanamo was a joint operation of the Islamic network and the intelligence agencies of Syria and Saudi Arabia. Alamoudi's National Muslim Prison Foundation trained the Muslim chaplains who worked in the U.S. armed forces, in our military prisons, and civilian jails, as we shall see in the next chapter.

CIA sources also told me that the mission at Guantanamo

was to learn the extent and nature of the information the United States had gained from "turned" prisoners and if it connected Syria to terrorist acts inside America. Had anyone named the names, or times, or places, that proves Syria's culpability beyond doubt?

The Arab world needs this information desperately because they are certain of one reality in the global politic: If such a link is established tracing responsibility back to Damascus for a major terrorist event like 9/11, the question won't be *will* the president of the United States take military action against Syria, it will be how soon.

CHAPTER 3

THE PRISON SYSTEM

On February 6, 2003, a furious New York governor George
Pataki put out the following press release:

The statements made by Warith Deen Umar are outrageous and
deplorable. New Yorkers, including our strong and vibrant Muslim
community, have tremendous respect for religious freedom, but
we will not tolerate any individual who supports or encourages
cowardly acts of terrorism or hatred or racism in any form.

Muslim prison chaplains were in the forefront following 9/11,
joining with chaplains of other faiths to prevent prison tensions
and to counsel inmates and staff alike that the cowardly attacks
were perpetrated by terrorists, not by any religion. In contrast,
Umar's outrageous comments are designed to heighten tension
and promote hatred and intolerance.

New Yorkers embrace religious freedom and diversity and we

will never allow dangerous and irresponsible individuals to divide us.[1]

Governor Pataki was referring to one Warith-Deen Umar, born Wallace Gene Marks, the former head Muslim chaplain of New York State prisons, whom the governor had banned from entering all the state's correctional facilities. Formerly calling himself "Wallace 10X," Umar found religion in jail as a teenager. He preached anti-Western radicalism to Muslim inmates, most of whom were converted while incarcerated, and led other Islamic chaplains to do the same.

Umar rose to be head Muslim chaplain of New York State Prisons and founder-president of the National Association of Muslim Chaplains, the perfect position to insert the Wahhabi doctrine of Islam into the prison system. PBS's flagship series *Frontline,* proud of its "credible, thoughtful reporting," said this about Wahhabism: "Strict Wahhabis believe that all those who don't practice their form of Islam are heathens and enemies."[2] Stephen Schwartz, in his book *The Two Faces of Islam,* wrote, "Wahabism exalts and promotes death in every element of its existence: the suicide of its adherents, mass murder as a weapon against civilization, and above all the suffocation of the mercy embodied in Islam."[3]

It wasn't hard for Umar to feed anti-Americanism to inmates already disenchanted with America. Their own country had impoverished them, but from Wahhabism emanated the not-so-faint smell of Saudi billions. The founder of the Prison Fellowship Ministries, Chuck Colson, confirms that Muslim chaplains are still hard at work recruiting in our nation's correctional facilities.

> Alienated, disenfranchised people are prime targets for radical Islamists who preach a religion of violence, of overcoming oppression by jihad. Yes, most Muslims interpret jihad as an inner struggle. But the radical fundamentalists—some of whom are invading our prisons—mean it literally. Those who take the Koran seriously are taught to hate the Christian and the Jew; lands taken from Islam must be recaptured. And to the Islamist, dying in a jihad is the only way one can be assured of Allah's forgiveness and eternal salvation.[4]

John Pistole, assistant director of the FBI Counterterrorism Division, testifying before the Senate Judiciary Committee, Subcommittee on Terrorism, Technology, and Homeland Security, on the FBI's role in preventing terrorist recruitment in correctional facilities, described Umar as "[a] Radical Muslim, [who] denied prisoners access to mainstream imams and materials. He sought to incite prisoners against America, preaching that the 9/11 hijackers should be remembered as martyrs and heroes."[5] Pistole was referring to Umar's remark at a public event: "Even Muslims who say they are against terrorism secretly admired and applauded [the September 11 hijackers]."[6]

However, according to the Imam Warith-Deen Umar Defense Committee hosted by the Bethlehem Neighbors for Peace Web site:

Imam Warith-Deen Umar, a resident of the Town of Bethlehem, NY, has led an exemplary life of devotion to his faith, to the struggle for social justice, and in support of his family and community. . . . This fight is not just for Umar's own rights but for the rights of all Muslims and of all people to speak the truth. Since the revelation that the FBI is spying on peace groups around the country, it has become clear that in order to defend our own rights, we must defend everyone's rights, including and especially the rights of the most vulnerable among us. Therefore, we members of the Bethlehem Neighbors for Peace have voted to support Imam Umar's fight, and we urge everyone to join us.[7]

It is a matter of record that al Qaeda recruiters in our prisons seek out men like Jose Padilla to convert to radical Islam. According to Colson, "Al Qaeda training manuals specifically identify America's prisoners as candidates for conversion because they may be 'disenchanted with their country's policies.' As U.S. citizens, they will combine a desire for 'payback' with an ability to blend easily into American culture."[8] A former gang member, Padilla had a long record of violence, with a hatred for America that proved easy to be nurtured by Militant Islam into acts of terrorism.

Padilla was born on October 18, 1970, and raised in a small stone building in the predominately Hispanic Logan Square neighborhood of Chicago. Although he is of Puerto Rican descent, government documents and criminal proceedings have also identified him as Latino, white, and black. Nicknamed

"Pucho" because of his chubby cheeks, Padilla attended St. Sylvester Catholic Church with his mother, two sisters, and a brother. That didn't stop Padilla from joining a mostly Puerto Rican street gang known as the Latin Disciples and soon after being convicted of aggravated battery and armed robbery, and sent off to a juvenile detention facility.

His stint in juvenile hall didn't help Padilla see the light, and he went on to commit a wide range of crimes. As an adult, he held down a string of menial, dead-end jobs. In the fall of 1991, he and his family headed to Florida. The warm climate didn't change what Chicago started. Padilla was arrested for a road-rage incident in which he fired a pistol at another driver.

After a stay in the Broward County Jail in 1992, Padilla got a job at a Taco Bell. Having a job gave Padilla new direction—it also gave him a friend and mentor. The manager of the Taco Bell was a Muslim Pakistani immigrant, Mohammad Javed Qureshi, co-founder of the Sunrise School of Islamic Studies. Padilla had been exposed to Islam in prison, and some reports say he converted in a Florida jail. Actually, incarceration was where his radicalization began. Qureshi built on that process and Padilla began to study with him to return to Islam.

Padilla's conversion came at a mosque in Sunrise, Florida, in 1994. Interestingly, the imam at the mosque at the time was Raed Awad, the reputed fund-raiser for the Holy Land Foundation for Relief and Development (HLF) in Florida.[9] On December 4, 2001, the Holy Land Foundation for Relief and Development, headquartered in Richardson, Texas, was placed in the category of "Specially Designated Global Terrorists" (SDGT) pursuant to the Order and Executive Order 12947 based on its support for Hamas.

By 1996 Padilla had taken to wearing a red-checkered *keffiyeh* headdress. In 1998, he moved to Egypt to learn Arabic and to deepen his understanding of Islam. Living in a suburb of Cairo, he adopted the name Abdullah al-Muhajir but became frustrated with what he felt was a secularized form of Islamic teachings available to him in Egypt, so he moved to Pakistan.

Before September 11, 2001, Padilla met Zayn al-Abidin Muhammed Husayn Abu Zubaydah, Osama bin Laden's chief of military operations for al Qaeda. Padilla became Abu Zubaydah's apprentice and traveled with him during 2001–2002 while Abu Zubaydah was reorganizing the remnants of the al Qaeda network scattered by the U.S. attacks on Afghanistan.

Among the new al Qaeda terrorist actions Abu Zubaydah was preparing was a plan to detonate a radiological weapon, or "dirty bomb," in the United States. In March 2002, Abu Zubaydah sent Padilla to meet al Qaeda leaders and to work with an associate constructing the bomb, but Abu Zubaydah was arrested just weeks later and turned over to U.S. authorities. Information obtained from Zubaydah led to Padilla's arrest at O'Hare International Airport after traveling from Pakistan to Zurich, then to Egypt, then back to Zurich, and then on to Chicago. He was carrying more than $10,000 in cash. According to Zubaydah, Padilla had been sent back to the States to find radioactive material that could be used to build a dirty bomb.

From a first exposure to radical Islam in prison to recruitment and training abroad, Padilla had come full circle—returning to America as an alleged al Qaeda terrorist whose target was his native country.

Inmate recruitment isn't just a problem in America. It is an international network of subversion, conversion, and recruitment, demonstrated by the attempt of British citizen and al Qaeda member Richard Colvin Reid to blow up American Airlines Flight 63—carrying 197 people from Paris to Miami with a crude bomb embedded in his sneaker on December 22, 2001.

Immediately dubbed the "Shoe Bomber" by the media, Reid was a third-generation British citizen, born in London in 1973. He was the only son of an English mother and a father of British-Jamaican ancestry who was in prison when his son was born.

Reid's parents divorced when he was thirteen, and he left school at sixteen, drifting into a variety of criminal activities not unlike his American counterpart Padilla. Arrested for mugging at seventeen, he spent the next six years in and out of jail, where he was first exposed to Islam and later converted to it. In 1995, he left prison and took the Arabic name Abdul-Raheem. At first his conversion to Islam appeared salutary, but he became estranged from family members after failing to convert them to his beliefs.

Reid's journey into Militant Islam intensified in 1997 when he began a relationship with radical Muslims, including Zacarias Moussaoui, who was later arrested and charged in the 9/11 attacks on the World Trade Center. Reid left his home and traveled to Pakistan and Afghanistan, where he trained at al Qaeda camps. He returned to London in the summer of 2001, only to return quickly to Pakistan and Afghanistan. During this time he visited Egypt, Turkey, and even tried to gain entry to Israel. After obtaining a new British passport, most likely to keep his travel patterns from the authorities, Reid was subdued trying to blow up Flight 63.

Padilla and Reid are excellent examples of what the secret Islamic network looks for—minority males, poor, uneducated, alienated, with a history of trouble with the law. They are often abandoned or isolated from friends and families. They are easily swayed and manipulated once they are converted to radical Islam.

There is an ample supply of these men throughout America's prison system, and in prisons throughout the world. In 2002, for the first time, the Justice Department estimated that more than 5.6 million Americans are in prison or have served time there. That translates into 1 in 37 adults living in this country. If this trend continues, 1 in 3 black males would serve time in prison. For Hispanics, it would be 1 in 6; and for whites, 1 in 17.[10]

Prisons are well known for exacerbating racial conflict. In my experience running a number of educational programs for the Correctional Educational Consortium at New York's Rikers Island facility in the 1980s, a high percentage of inmates view "white" society as their oppressor and America's "racist legal system" as responsible for their incarceration. These beliefs cause racial confrontations throughout jails and prisons across the country. Even inmates who aren't racist soon become so as a cycle of hatred and violence between inmates draws them in.

In the violent closed world of a correctional setting, identifying with a group means survival. It can save your life. Friends protect; they watch our backs. Your enemy is their enemy. There is unity and strength in belonging to a group, especially if the group provides physical—and spiritual—protection. Islamic groups inside prisons deliver just that—protection.

Significant numbers of minority inmates seek out Islam for just that reason. Many converts enrolled in my programs told me that Islam helped them escape the violence of prison life. It was true that some converted for the more palatable halal food products, but the overwhelming majority did so for safety.

Safe passage had a price, however—proselytizing that bordered on brainwashing. Constant discussions of racism and strife ruled the day. If an individual under my supervision wasn't convinced of how "bad" this country was before his conversion, he was certainly convinced after conversion, listening to fellow Muslims constantly listing the evils of American society. It added religious righteousness to the condemnation of the racist system that caused their incarceration. Time and time again, I heard converts discussing how Islam set them free from the racism of America—and gave them the right to fight back.

The nonviolent methods of Martin Luther King Jr. had no place in their discussions. To me, they were the dangerous teachings of Frantz Fanon, expressed in his *The Wretched of the*

Earth.[11] Fanon, a black psychiatrist, posited that only through spilling the blood of oppressors could the downtrodden destroy their masters and in the process feel good about themselves. He justified violence. So did Islam's teachings in the prisons, as I was exposed to it.

The National Islamic Prison Foundation claims to convert 135,000 prisoners a year. Jane I. Smith, a recognized authority on Islam in prison, puts the number at 30,000.[12] Either figure is substantial, and reportedly growing every year. On a positive note, many of these conversions are shepherded by Muslims practicing traditional nonviolent Islamic beliefs. However, there are others who preach a virulent form of the religion—radical clerics who take advantage of the racism and violence within prisons to continue their own form of violence and hatred.

Sulayman Nyang, professor of African Studies at Howard University in Washington, D.C., and the lead developer for the African Voices Project of the Museum of Natural History of the Smithsonian Institution, estimated that 1 out of every 10 African American Muslims came to Islam through a prison conversion.[13]

On March 10, 2003, the Office of the Inspector General (OIG) of the Department of Justice began to take a hard look at that. It was also prompted by New York Senator Charles Schumer, who wrote to them, concerned about the Federal Bureau of Prisons' use of Islamic groups to endorse Muslim chaplains—the Islamic Society of North America (ISNA) and the Graduate School of Islamic and Social Sciences (GSISS).

Schumer and Senators Jon Kyl of Arizona and Dianne Feinstein of California expressed their concerns that these organizations were connected to terrorism and positioned to promote
Wahhabism.[14]

After 9/11, the ISNA and the GSISS were far more closely
scrutinized by the government. According to the U.S. Attorney's Office for the Eastern District of Virginia, the GSISS has
been under federal investigation since December 2001 for providing support to terrorists. Several of the ISNA board members were accused of supporting or having ties to terrorism.
One ISNA board member Siraj Wahhaj was named by Mary
Jo White, former U.S. attorney for the Southern District of
New York, as one of the unindicted persons who may be an alleged co-conspirator in the 1993 World Trade Center bombing.
Another ISNA board member, Bassam Osman, heads the
North American Islamic Trust (NAIT), which reportedly owns
the Islamic Academy of Florida—which a federal indictment
handed down last year accused of raising funds for the terrorist
organization Palestinian Islamic Jihad.[15]

In April 2004, an OIG report titled "A Review of the Bureau
of Prisons' Selection of Muslim Religious Services Providers"
identified the following problems related to the selection of
Muslim religious service providers:

> the BOP typically does not examine the doctrinal beliefs of ap-
> plicants for religious service positions to determine whether those
> beliefs are inconsistent with BOP security policies;

the BOP and the FBI have not adequately exchanged information regarding the BOP's Muslim endorsing organizations;

because the BOP currently has no national Islamic organizations willing or able to provide endorsements for its Muslim chaplains candidates, the BOP's hiring of new Muslim chaplains is effectively frozen, resulting in a shortage of Muslim chaplains within the BOP;

the BOP does not effectively use the expertise of its current Muslim chaplains to screen, recruit, and supervise Muslim religious service providers;

once contractors and certain volunteers gain access to BOP facilities, ample opportunity exists for them to deliver inappropriate and extremist messages without supervision from BOP staff members;

BOP inmates often lead Islamic religious services, subject only to intermittent supervision from BOP staff members, which enhances the likelihood that inappropriate content can be delivered to inmates.

Within the BOP's chapels, significant variations exist in the level of supervision provided by correctional officers.[16]

The OIG report exposes serious flaws in how Muslim service providers are vetted and controlled once inside the 105 BOP facilities nationwide. The only method the BOP uses to screen chaplain candidates' beliefs is the Candidate Certification and Authorization, a signed pledge that the chaplain will minister to inmates of all faiths. The chief of the Chaplaincy Services Branch of the Federal Bureau of Prisons seems comfortable with the investigative scope of requiring a pledge. The OIG report quotes her as saying that Muslims with extreme Islamic views, like Wahhabism, and those who encourage violence against Christians and Jews, "would not be willing to sign this statement, *unless they were attempting to infiltrate the prisons by misrepresenting their beliefs* [emphasis added]."[17] Her assumption: they would not lie unless they would infiltrate.

The BOP does not ask candidates whether they have received funds from foreign governments. In addition, the BOP will not hire a chaplain candidate who has spent a significant amount of time in a country that does not have diplomatic relations or treaties with the United States, but she did not define how much time precluded hiring.[18]

The BOP provides Muslim inmates with religious services through BOP chaplains, contractors, and volunteers. Since 2001 ten chaplains, or a little more than 4 percent of the BOP's total chaplains, are Muslim. According to the BOP, it currently is experiencing a critical shortage of Muslim chaplains. When a Muslim chaplain is not available in a prison, Muslim inmates' religious services are provided by Muslim volunteers, contractors, or inmates.[19]

Muslim contractors are compensated by the BOP to provide certain Islamic services to inmates. Volunteers are not compensated. As of September 6, 2003, there were 56 Muslim contractors and 108 Muslim Level 2 volunteers; no information on the number of Level 1 volunteers was provided in the OIG report:

> Unlike chaplains and contractors, volunteers are not required to pass a drug screening urinalysis or provide contact information for their employers for the past five years. They also are not asked to report the professional, civic, and religious organizations in which they hold membership or whether they have received funds from foreign governments. Ex-offenders are eligible to serve as volunteers, but must have no arrests for three or more years after their release, must submit to a background check in which they provide and verify their current employment or academic status, and cannot be placed in a prison that houses inmates who have separation orders against them. The BOP does not screen volunteers' doctrinal beliefs or require they provide a statement of faith. The BOP also does not consult their own BOP Muslim chaplains regarding the screening of Muslim volunteers, or ask its chaplains to gather information from the local community or volunteer applicants. The Chief of the Chaplaincy Services Branch told the OIG that she believed it would be beneficial for chaplains to examine volunteers' activities and reputations in their communities and religious congregations.[20]

According to the FBI, it is likely that terrorist groups such as al Qaeda will attempt to radicalize and recruit inmates in the United States. An Ohio State correctional official reported radicalization had led some inmates in state prisons to become members of terrorist groups, including the Islamic militant group Hezbollah and the Irish Republican Army.[21] An FBI counterterrorism analyst told the OIG that the immense wealth associated with Saudi Wahhabism makes the religion especially appealing to inmates who are seeking financial support and assistance after they leave prison.

Unfortunately, the OIG report also confirms that almost three years after 9/11, federal agencies are still not sharing information. "The FBI and the BOP have not effectively exchanged information about endorsing organizations' possible connections to terrorism. In our view, these and other practices identified in this report create unnecessary risks to prison and national security."[22]

At a time that we should be watching the prison system with a sharp eye on what it's creating, the ACLU is trying its best to support some of those individuals, many with frightening records. For example, here are sections of a brief submitted by the ACLU:

Frank Askin, Esq.

Rutgers Constitutional Litigation Clinic

123 Washington Street

Newark, New Jersey 07102

(973) 353-5687

Attorney for Plaintiffs on Behalf

of the American Civil Liberties Union

Foundation of New Jersey

NEW JERSEY STATE	)SUPERIOR COURT OF
CONFERENCE – NAACP, THE	)NEW JERSEY
LATINO LEADERSHIP ALLIANCE	)UNION COUNTY
OF NEW JERSEY, . . .	)CHANCERY DIVISION

CIVIL ACTION

COMPLAINT

PRELIMINARY STATEMENT

1. This case challenges New Jersey's practice of denying suffrage to convicted persons on parole and probation and the resulting discriminatory impact that such denial of suffrage has on the African-American and Hispanic electorate in the State.

PARTIES

6. Plaintiff TS, who resides [in] New Jersey, is an African-American of lawful voting age, a citizen of the United States and a legal resident of New Jersey. He is currently on parole and thus pursuant to N.J.S.A. 19:4-1 (8), is not entitled to vote. Mr. STRICKLAND has been on parole since his release from Rahway State Prison in 2002, and will remain on parole until 2006. Despite his criminal history, Mr. Strickland states that he has been a law-abiding citizen since joining the Nation of Islam and taking its "Life Skills" training course while incarcerated. He is an active member of Nation of Islam Mosque No. 85 in New Brunswick, New Jersey, and performs voluntary field work for the Mosque. He has been employed since his release from prison, and he filed his first tax return for the year 2002.

In Muslim countries, the theocratic government sanctions religious leaders who will minister to inmates. The United States, however, has allowed foreign-born Muslims to come and create their own organizations to endorse the credentials of Muslim chaplains. The danger lies in what the secret Islamic network has been doing for twenty years, and what it continues to do—connecting its subversive enterprises to the larger purpose and plan of Militant Islam worldwide.

Abdurahman Muhammad Alamoudi is key to understanding this nexus. His affiliation with Washington politicians, and the fortune he controlled, concealed the purpose of his national Muslim organizations—as they concealed Alamoudi's laundering Libyan money through Saudi banks to finance political activities in Washington to create Muslim organizations to vet imams for American prisons where they would recruit and radicalize converts to Islam.

Concealed within the schools that Alamoudi built was yet another tentacle of the secret network. The Graduate School of Islamic and Social Sciences, run by prominent Islamic scholar Taha Jabir al-Alwani, is one of the Islamic organizations that endorse Muslim chaplains for the military.[23] At least seven of the twelve Muslim chaplains in the armed forces were educated at GSISS.[24]

In March 2002, al-Alwani's home and a network of interlocking Islamic nonprofit groups and businesses in suburban Virginia were raided by a Customs Service task force searching for evidence of funneled money to groups like al Qaeda and the Palestinian Islamic Jihad. The search warrants tied al-Alwani to Sami al-Arian—one of the original "Mullahs" from North Carolina who used the World and Islam Studies Enterprise and the Islamic Concern Project as fronts to raise money in America for Militant Islamic organizations.[25] No charges have been filed against al-Alwani.

Alamoudi founded not only national Muslim organizations but, working with the Pentagon for nearly a decade, he was able to create the American Muslim Armed Forces and Veterans Affairs Council. Through them he was able to insert Muslim chaplains into the ranks of the U.S. military and later into the military prison in Guantanamo.

In 1993, through his National Muslim Prison Foundation, the same Alamoudi spearheaded efforts to install radical Muslim chaplains inside prisons throughout the United States. "The purpose, counterterrorism experts say, was to take over Islamic chaplain programs and install more militant Muslims to indoctrinate inmates inside the U.S. prison system and network them after their release back into society."[26]

It was only after Alamoudi's arrest in 2003 that government officials questioned the nation's method of screening Muslim chaplains for sensitive positions. Arizona Republican Senator Jon Kyl said point-blank that the Pentagon's review of all its chaplains was "the height of politically correct stupidity."[27]

Muslim organizations currently vetting Muslim chaplains are also under investigation. The Islamic Society of North America is the oldest of these organizations and the only one that filed the necessary paperwork required by the BOP to endorse the qualifications of Muslim chaplains. Congress is reviewing the

society's financial records as part of its investigation into alleged ties between certain tax-exempt Muslim organizations and
terrorist groups.[28]

The Islamic Assembly of North America (IANA), incorporated as a nonprofit organization to promote Islam, is alleged to
have funneled money to finance terrorism.[29] Its ranks are filled
with a host of unsavory characters tied to radical Islam. One of
its founding members, Bassem K. Khafagi—who was also community affairs director of the Council on American-Islamic Relations at the time of his arrest—pled guilty last year to charges
of bank and visa fraud. IANA is also affiliated with a New York–
based nonprofit called Help the Needy, which itself is under
investigation by the FBI for possible terrorist links.[30]

Many believe the Islamic Circle of North America (ICNA)
to have ties to the Muslim Brotherhood, the ideological foundation of Militant Islamic movements, including Hamas and al
Qaeda. Terrorism expert Steven Emerson writes: "ICNA
openly supports militant Islamic fundamentalist organizations,
praises terror attacks, issues incendiary attacks on western values and policies, and supports the imposition of Sharia [Is-
lamic code of law]."[31]

The Office of the Inspector General's report "A Review of
the Federal Bureau of Prisons' Selection of Muslim Religious
Services Providers" concludes with a warning that we would do
well to heed:

> The presence of extremist chaplains, contractors, or volunteers in
> the BOP's correctional facilities can pose a threat to institutional

security and could implicate national security if inmates are encouraged to commit terrorist acts against the United States. For this reason, it is imperative that the BOP has in place sound screening and supervision practices that will identify persons who seek to disrupt the order of its institutions or to inflict harm on the United States through terrorism.[32]

CHAPTER 4

MOSQUES

Americans accustomed to the traditional concept of a clergy-man performing many different functions within the spiritual life of their congregations—counseling, ministering, interacting with family life, providing comfort—find it difficult to understand the role of imam. In a traditional mosque it is simply that of a prayer leader. Throughout the world, most imams have been trained in the Middle East, most often at Saudi Arabia's Imam Muhammad Ibn Saud Islamic University located in Riyadh.

The school is the largest Wahhabi university in the world, with branches in Washington, D.C.; Tokyo; Indonesia; Djibouti; and the United Arab Emirates (UAE). It wields global influence and is still expanding its reach. In the appendix is a letter from Saad al-Buraik, a senior adviser to Prince Abdul Aziz bin Fahd, son of King Fahd and minister of the royal court recommending the establishment of a new school in Japan that will be attached to the university (see the appendix).

It is also worth noting that two, and possibly as many as nine, of the university's graduates were 9/11 hijackers. In January 2004, the U.S. State Department revoked the diplomatic visas of sixteen people affiliated with the Institute for Islamic and Arabic Sciences in America in Fairfax, Virginia, a satellite campus of the university, following accusations that it was promoting a brand of Islam that is intolerant of Christianity, Judaism, and other religions.

It is therefore not surprising that imams in America are often conservative religious figures who find themselves at odds with their more Americanized congregations and are often out on the fringe, making inflammatory statements. Mohammed Gemeaha, the Egyptian-born imam of the Islamic Cultural Center in New York, suggested shortly after September 11, 2001, and before he resigned to go back to Egypt, that Israeli forces were behind the attack. In later comments to an Arabic-language Website, he said Jewish doctors in the United States were poisoning Muslim babies.[1] After diplomats from Egypt and Kuwait, the countries that paid for the $17 million mosque designed by the architectural firm Skidmore, Owings & Merrill, denounced his comments, the mosque leadership replaced Gemeaha with Palestinian Omar Abu Namous. Namous is quoted by Gersh Kuntzman, a columnist for the *New York Post,* in an article written shortly after 9/11. Considering what appeared to be the impending capture of Osama bin Laden, Kuntzman asked Namous what Mohammed would suggest be done to him. "If it is deliberate murder and the victims' families do not forgive the murderer, then the murderer must be killed," said Namous. "The traditional method, going back to the days of the prophet, is to be beheaded with a sword."[2] Regardless of Islam's claims of nonviolence, we see this tradition is still alive and well.

It's not just what's being said during Islamic services and sermons that reflect the extremist influence in America's Islamic institutions. The youngest members of Islamic society are being exposed to intolerance and hate in the Islamic religious schools from the earliest grades on. In 1997, there were over a hundred Islamic day schools and more than a thousand Sunday or weekend schools in the United States, many of them affiliated with mosques, all expanding the reach of Wahhabi doctrine.

For years, mainstream America wasn't watching what was taught in Islamic religious schools, but 9/11 put these learning institutions in the spotlight. The USA Patriot Act allowed the government to look into mosques for the first time. What investigators found was very disturbing. The Saudis, either directly or through intermediary groups such as the World Assembly of Muslim Youth (WAMY), are pouring "truckloads" of oil money into American mosques and schools, New York Democratic Senator Charles Schumer told a congressional subcommittee. "In exchange, they demand that these mosques and schools toe the Wahhabi line. Saudi textbooks that preach violence against infidels can be found in some American Muslim schools."[3]

In February 2003, the American Jewish Committee and the Center for Monitoring the Impact of Peace released an analysis of ninety-three textbooks published by the Saudi Ministry of Education and used between 1999 and 2002. The books, American Jewish Committee Executive Director David A. Harris told a congressional committee, "reveal a widespread presence of contempt towards Western civilization and followers of other religions."[4]

According to the study, the teachings include:

Islam is the only true religion.

Saudi Arabia is the leader of the Muslim world.

Christians and Jews are infidels.

The West is a "decaying society" and the source of Muslim misfortunes.

There can be no peace between Muslims and non-Muslims.

Jews are wicked.

Israel does not exist on world maps.[5]

Among the passages cited in the study is this one from a Saudi tenth-grade literary study book:

The Muslims will never get Palestine, or other [regions] back without holy Jihad by which faithful throngs will march and fight, so that God's word shall be the highest. And I do not think there will be among us one who will refrain from answering such a faithful call.[6]

Another Arabic literature book for tenth graders teaches, "There are two happy endings for Jihad fighters in God's cause: victory or martyrdom."[7]

It is of little comfort that, in defense of the books, Saudi Foreign Minister Saud al-Faisal told CBS's *60 Minutes* that "85 percent of what was being taught in the schools was not hateful."[8]

It isn't surprising that Islamic schools in the United States use Saudi textbooks. In fact, the textbook publisher, IQRA International Educational Foundation of Chicago, receives financial support from a Saudi foundation. But hate speech doesn't have to be imported. Investigations by several newspapers show that some of the most troubling books are produced right in the United States. In 2003 the New York *Daily News* took a look at textbooks with titles like *What Islam Is All About* and *Mercy to Mankind,* which were widely used in the city schools and were described by Islamic educational experts as among the most popular.[9]

The newspaper found that fifth and sixth graders at one school were being taught that "the Jews killed their own prophets and disobeyed Allah," while at another elementary school, students reading from *What Islam Is All About* learned that "the Christians also worship statues."[10] The book, which the publisher, the Islamic Foundation of North America of Queens, New York, says has sold more than forty thousand copies, also says that many Jews and Christians lead "decadent and immoral lives."[11]

The *Washington Post* found similar troubling textbooks and teachings at the Islamic academies in the Washington area. One eleventh-grade textbook says that a sign of the "Day of Judgment will be that Muslims will fight and kill Jews, who will hide behind talking trees that say: Oh Muslim, Oh servant of

God, here is a Jew hiding behind me. Come here and kill him."[12] Students are also taught in Islamic studies that it is good to dislike Christians, Jews, and Shiite Muslims.

There are many other possibly troubling links between Islamic education and terrorism. The Web site of the Council of Islamic Schools in North America (CISNA) contains a link to the Muslim Student Association, one of more than two dozen Muslim charities and foundations listed in a January 2004 Senate Finance Committee request to the Internal Revenue Service for confidential tax and financial records. The inquiry is part of a probe into alleged ties between the groups and terrorist organizations.

Another academic organization raising concerns is the Institute for Islamic and Arabic Sciences in America (IIASA). The institute, in Fairfax, Virginia, was established in 1998 and is affiliated with Al-Imam Muhammad Ibn Saud Islamic University in Riyadh, Saudi Arabia, which the Saudi Institute considers a conduit for Saudi-based hate literature in the United States.[13]

The IIASA teaches Wahhabism to over four hundred students, and is "beyond reform," Washington, D.C., Saudi Institute Director Ali al-Ahmed said in 2002. "It practices religious and gender apartheid. Female students are not allowed in the library except for four hours each week, when men are not around. Classes are segregated and women are taught through closed-circuit television."[14]

A common thread emerges from recent cases brought against confirmed or alleged Islamic terror cells in the United States—

the connection between the terror cell's members and a local mosque.

The six men of the al Qaeda sleeper cell in Lackawanna, New York, arrested by the FBI in 2001 for attending an al Qaeda terrorist training camp in Afghanistan all belonged to a Lackawanna mosque. One of the six, Sahim Alwan, was the former president of the Lackawanna Islamic Mosque.

The Lackawanna 6 case confirms our fears about mosques: The six men who grew up in the Yemeni community in Lackawanna were recruited by Kamal Derwish, a Yemeni American who was teaching about Islam in a mosque. Derwish was a Muslim extremist born in Buffalo but raised in Saudi Arabia. Derwish began the process of recruiting the men for al Qaeda during evening religious instruction. "Derwish would tell them: 'You don't even know the prophets, you won't make it past Judgment Day,'" said Rodney O. Personius, a former federal prosecutor who represented one of the six defendants. "Juma said that Mecca wouldn't do, that they needed jihad training if they wanted to save their souls."[15]

Later he brought in an imam named Juma al-Dosari, who FBI officials say was an al Qaeda recruiter. Al-Dosari worked at the Islamic Center in Bloomington, Indiana, but left in 2000 and was traveling in the United States when Derwish called him to come to Lackawanna. Derwish introduced al-Dosari to the six recruits as an old friend who had fought beside him in Bosnia and Chechnya.

Al-Dosari held classes with the six recruits at the mosque after evening prayers. He stressed that even a pilgrimage to

Mecca wasn't sufficient commitment to Islam—they had to train for Jihad. His words obviously convinced them. A short time after al-Dosari left Lackawanna for Saudi Arabia, the recruits left for Afghanistan and Osama bin Laden's terrorist academy, Al-Farouk, near Kandahar.

All six Lackawanna recruits have since pled guilty to giving material support to terrorism and were sentenced to seven to ten years in prison. Kamal Derwish was killed in 2002 in a car attack in Yemen by a missile from a CIA Predator drone meant for an al Qaeda member believed to be one of the planners of the deadly attack on the USS *Cole*.

Juma al-Dosari was captured on the Pakistan-Afghanistan border by guards a month after 9/11 and turned over to U.S. forces. He continues to be held at the detention center in Guantanamo Bay, Cuba. Federal agents in Indiana are still investigating whether al-Dosari might also have recruited Jihadists from among the young Muslims he worked with at Indiana University and Purdue University.

The Islamic Center of Portland, a Sunni mosque in suburban Beaverton, Oregon, also known as Masjed As-Saber, was the meeting ground for six members indicted by federal authorities in 2002 for conspiring to provide aid to the Taliban and al Qaeda terrorists. FBI's Portland Joint Terrorism Task Force also arrested the imam of the mosque, Sheik Mohamed Abdirahman Kariye, as he was preparing to leave the country with his family.

FBI documents allege that Kariye used $12,000 collected from members of the mosque to fund the efforts of the "Portland 6" to join the Taliban. Kariye ultimately pleaded guilty to unrelated federal fraud charges and received probation.[16]

A second Oregon mosque, the Bilal Mosque, also in Beaverton, has been connected to several people of interest to federal investigators. Two members of the "Portland 6"—brothers Ahmed Ibrahim Bilal and Muhammad Ibrahim Bilal—collected thousands of dollars from worshipers at the mosque by claiming they needed money to help their parents in Saudi Arabia. In reality, it was to finance their trip to join the Taliban.[17]

The Al-Farooq Mosque in Brooklyn, New York, has been in the public spotlight for more than a decade, since the time that Sheik Omar Abdel-Rahman, the blind Egyptian-born cleric convicted in 1995 of conspiracy to bomb New York City landmarks, was imam there. During a relatively short time as imam, Abdel-Rahman was vociferous in calling for Jihad against the enemies of Islam. In March 2003, U.S. Attorney General John Ashcroft said that one of two Yemeni men arrested as fundraisers for al Qaeda and Hamas terrorist groups, Al Hasan al-Moayad, had bragged to an FBI informant that he had personally delivered $20 million to Osama bin Laden. Some money, al-Moayad said, was collected at the Al-Farooq Mosque.[18]

Abdel-Rahman was also a regular speaker at the Al-Salaam

mosque in Jersey City, New Jersey, where many of the suspects in the 1993 World Trade Center bombing worshiped. During his tenure at the Jersey City mosque, Abdel-Rahman issued regular calls for the violent overthrow of the Egyptian government and other Arab regimes. Tape recordings of his sermons were smuggled into Egypt.

In 2003, Amin Awad, a Muslim chaplain who counsels inmates in New York's Rikers Island jail, was reassigned because of his affiliation to the Al-Farooq Mosque that authorities still believe is linked to terrorist fund-raising. Just prior to his reassignment, Awad was named president of the board of trustees at the storefront mosque.[19]

American mosques are regular stops on fund-raising trips for terrorist leaders and their sympathizers. Osama bin Laden's chief deputy, Ayman al-Zawahiri, made at least two money-raising trips to the United States in the early 1990s, according to testimony from a man who pleaded guilty to conspiracy charges in relation to the two deadly African embassy bombings in 1998. A California newspaper reported two members of a terrorist cell in that state had helped him with a stolen passport and a fake name. He visited at least three mosques in California—in Santa Clara, Stockton, and Sacramento—during a national fund-raising tour. Another convicted money smuggler, Alaa al-Saadawi, admitted raising funds for the Global Relief Foundation, an Illinois-based Islamic charity on the government's list of organizations financing terrorism.[20] His lawyer claimed al-Saadawi was collecting contributions in a lawful effort to build new mosques and schools in the United States.

In a November 2003 hearing on Saudi intolerance conducted by the U.S. Commission on International Religious Freedom, a group established by Congress to make recommendations to the president, Chairman Michael Young warned of a growing number of reports that funding coming from Saudi Arabia has been used to finance religious schools and other activities that support the kind of hate, intolerance, and violence practiced by Islamic militants and extremists in several parts of the world."[21]

Consider the speech given by Saudi cleric Shaikh Saad al-Buraik at a government mosque in Riyadh in 2002. Al-Buraik was the host of a forty-eight-hour telethon that raised $109 million for Palestinian fighters and the families of "martyrs." On the tape, translated by the Saudi Institute in Washington, D.C., al-Buraik calls for Jewish women to be enslaved:

"Muslim Brothers in Palestine, do not have any mercy neither compassion on the Jews, their blood, their money, their flesh. Their women are yours to take, legitimately. God made them yours. Why don't you enslave their women? Why don't you wage jihad? Why don't you pillage them?"

On Jihad:

"Which is better to suffer—a slow death, or to die as a martyr on your way to heaven? A death that you will be forgiven on the first drop of your blood."

"Which is a better choice, to die on your bed, or to die per-severant, fighting, not retreating. Which is better to suffer—long before death many days, or taste death quickly?"

And on America:

"I am against America until this life ends, until the Day of Judgment."

"She is the root of all evils, and wickedness on earth."

"I am against America even if the stone liquefies."

"My hatred of America, if part of it was contained in the universe, it would collapse."

Al-Buraik is now the host of his own TV show, *Religion and Life,* on Saudi government television Channel One.

What does al-Buraik's speech mean to Americans? Is it more than just words from a fanatic thousands of miles from our borders? It's far more: the centerpiece of a trail that leads to terrorism on our shores.

The tape has been widely distributed with the Arabic title *A Monkey Desecrates a Mosque.* The title is clearly anti-Semitic given the cover art (see the appendix). The back cover gives (in Arabic) the copyright as belonging to the World Assembly of Moslem Youth, an organization founded by Abdullah bin Laden, a nephew of Osama bin Laden.[22]

According to its Web site, "WAMY is the first International Islamic Organization dealing specially with youth affairs embracing over 450 Islamic youth/students organization in the five continents. WAMY has 66 branches and representatives, over 500 member organizations and a worldwide network for the implementation of its programs."[23]

Although WAMY was expelled from Pakistan—and both Pakistan and India alleged that WAMY was funding a group linked to attacks in Kashmir—and the Philippines military accused it of funding Muslim insurgency,[24] WAMY operates freely in the United States. Their office's mailing address is in Falls Church, Virginia.

On September 17, 2003, Senator Chuck Schumer sent a letter to Attorney General John Ashcroft asking for an investigation of WAMY based on the following:

> . . . there is substantial evidence suggesting that the World Assembly of Muslim Youth, an Islamic organization that operates out of Virginia, participates in terrorist financing.
>
> Reports show that WAMY serves as a major conduit for Saudi Arabian financing of the terrorist group Hamas.
>
> Hamas' spiritual leader, Sheik Ahmed Yassin, publicly thanked WAMY for its continued support in a speech he delivered in Gaza.
>
> Arab press reports indicate that WAMY spends $2.7 million annually in support of the Palestinian Intifada, in addition to $70 million it has collected in donations for this purpose at WAMY offices worldwide.[25]

The secret Islamic terror network inside the United States is evident when one connects these dots: hate speech from a Wahhabi government cleric in a Saudi Arabian government mosque is copyrighted by WAMY, a Saudi-based organization called "a major conduit for Saudi Arabian financing of the terrorist group Hamas"; WAMY is constructing 123 mosques around the world, with 103 more under construction (see the appendix); Saudi Arabia is building or operating hundreds of mosques in America and opening branches of Saudi universities here to train imams; WAMY collects money in the USA; and according to Senator Jon Kyl, "a growing body of accepted evidence and expert research demonstrates that the Wahabi ideology that dominates, finances and animates many groups here in the United States, indeed, is antithetical to the values of tolerance, individualism and freedom as we conceive these things."[26]

The dots lead here: America is cooperating in its own destruction if it continues to let Saudi-dominated Wahhabi mosques control Islam's agenda, and Americans will be financing terrorism within America unless it stops groups like WAMY from operating and freely collecting money here.

It isn't an accident that many U.S. mosques have become appendages of worldwide Jihad against the West. The number of Muslims coming here rose rapidly after the United States revised immigration laws in the mid-1960s. The number of mosques and Islamic community centers grew over that time, by some estimates from about fifty at the end of World War II to more than twelve hundred today.

The role of the mosque has also changed—from Americanized "cultural clubs" of earlier immigrants to conservative, religion-oriented institutions that manipulate the national and cultural identities of new immigrants in an effort to avoid their inclusion in mainstream America.

Mosques cost money. More often than not, it comes from Saudi Arabia—or, in the case of Shi'a mosques, from Iran. The Saudis built more than 60 percent in the 1980s and 1990s. By one estimate, by 2002 the Saudis had spent more than $70 billion to fund 80 percent of the mosques built in the United States in the last 20 years.

According to one Saudi Website, as of 2003 the Kingdom of Saudi Arabia has built more than two hundred Islamic centers in Europe, America, Australia, Africa, and Asia. This includes the Islamic Cultural Center on the Upper East Side of New York and mosques in Los Angeles, Washington, Chicago, Maryland, Ohio, and Virginia.[27]

The Los Angeles mosque, the Bilal Islamic Center, was one of the addresses given by Mark Fidel Kools, also known as Asan Akbar, the 101st Airborne Sergeant who killed a fellow serviceman and wounded fifteen others with a grenade in Kuwait shortly after the Iraq war began in March 2003. According to the *Los Angeles Times,* soldiers who witnessed Akbar's arrest said that Akbar yelled, "You guys are coming into our countries, and you're going to rape our women and kill our children."[28]

"It's very difficult for American Muslims to collect enough money to build their own mosques, and so they rely on these institutions," said Harvard University professor of Arabic Language and Literature Ahmed al-Rahim at an Ethics and Public Policy Center panel in Washington, D.C., in 2003. "That reliance brings political baggage with it, as mosques become subservient to an entire political program, a very radical political program."[29]

Journalist and author William McGowan says in his book *Coloring the News:* "The journalistic mainstream has also been reluctant to do the investigative work required to establish that mosques are not being used in some cases as recruiting grounds or sanctuaries for terrorists, even though the FBI has shown that past terror plotters used such houses of worship for those purposes."[30]

Proving mosques are part of the fifth column in America is not hard. Militant Islam is operating in mosques all over the world. Abu Hamza al-Masri has led the well-known mosque at Finsbury Park in north London since 1996. Al-Masri, a Mujahideen who lost both hands and an eye in an explosion in Afghanistan, recruited young Muslims to go to Afghanistan to be trained as Jihadists.

Al-Masri has railed against almost every aspect of American foreign policy and was quoted recently as saying, "Bin Laden is a good guy. Everyone likes him in the Muslim world, there is nothing wrong with the man and his beliefs. Many people will be happy, jumping up and down [after September 11]. America is a crazy superpower and what was done was done in self-defense."[31]

The combination of radical Islamic brainwashing and Jihadist training in terror camps has proved lethal for the United

States more than once. "Shoe Bomber" Richard Reid, Zacarias Moussaoui—the first person indicted in the United States for the 9/11 attack on the World Trade Center—and the recruiters of Nizar Trabelsi, the professional German soccer player turned al Qaeda suicide bomber jailed for planning to blow up an American military base in Belgium—were all connected to the Finsbury Park mosque.

The Afghan camps were the final step in creating terrorists, as described in Moussaoui's own words:

Once in the camp, it is easy, as in any sect to make him lose his bearings. First of all he is put through athletic training, and then training in weapon handling. These are intensive exercises. He is always being set challenges that are increasingly difficult to meet. The young recruit is not well fed. He gradually becomes exhausted. He never manages to completely come up with what is being asked of him. After several weeks or months, he gets the feeling that he's not capable of doing what is expected of him. He experiences a feeling of embarrassment and malaise. In his own eyes, he is completely belittled: he feels guilty because he is incompetent. And yet he is told over and over again that others before him have succeeded and gone on to great things. . . . And if he carries on, it is to the bitter end. Because the only thing he can do to help the cause is to give his life to it. And this will also prove to others that, at the end, he met their expectations. He is now ripe for suicide.[32]

During the winter of 2004, a former CIA agent with a direct pipeline to Homeland Security arranged for me to have a combined briefing from a group of federal security, intelligence, and law-enforcement agencies in Washington, D.C. My briefing group can be identified only as including career CIA officers who had worked inside Syria and Iran; a State Department officer previously stationed in the Middle East, now with the FBI; government security experts; and several others with long experience in intelligence and foreign service.

In attendance was a quiet, casually dressed Middle Eastern man in his fifties. According to our hosts, he was the "real deal." He regularly frequented mosques and knew the imams and the worshipers. He was Special Ops and a demolitions expert. He knew terrorists. He had infiltrated their organizations; he had killed terrorists before they could strike innocents.

However, when the briefing turned to mosques as a source of terrorist activity and incendiary rhetoric, he completely downplayed the role of mosques in the lives of both legal and illegal Muslims. I said he was wrong, that most mosques glorify Muslim martyrs, with their imams extolling violence until, coupled with distortions of the Koran and Islamic law, killing nonbelievers is more than virtuous, it is mandatory. I also maintained that mosques called for money from members to support captured terrorists. I offered to show him the document from a Jersey City mosque posted by the "Defense Committee: Ali El Gabroni and Manmoud Abuhaima," asking for money to give aid to our beloved brothers who were wrongfully accused of the World Trade Center incident. These are pious, Allah fearing individuals (Muhammad Salamah, Niddal Ayyad, Mahmoud Abu-halima, Balai Al-Khasy and Ibrahim El-Gabrowny) who became victims of conspiracy and bias.

The men listed above weren't "victims of conspiracy and bias." Every one was convicted in court on various counts of the 1993 bombing of the World Trade Center. They were terrorists. They murdered American citizens. The Middle Eastern man said no such activities were occurring in any mosque that he knew and denied even the possibility that mosques advanced Militant Islam's political agendas, or played a role in terrorism, or provided money to terrorists or their supporters.

My briefing team agreed with him—Militant Islam was a relatively small threat. If that was so, I asked, how did they account for the daily acts of terrorism and suicide bombings by religious fanatics. One said without hesitation, "Go meet Pat Robertson and Jerry Falwell if you want to see what *real* fanatics are like." Another said, "Compared to them, maybe the Islamic ones aren't so bad after all."

It was insulting to me, to the patriotism of the men mentioned, and to every American passionate about the safety of America. How much of this kind of attitude had led to our current problems?

The briefing in Washington confirmed for me that our intelligence experts don't understand the nature of terrorism in the twenty-first century. That means they will continue to give incorrect advice to those who formulate American policy and those who carry it out. As a result, Militant Islam will only grow more powerful—and the threat of harm to American citizens more likely.

CHAPTER 5

THE DRUG CONNECTION

In a speech to the Organized Crime and Drug Enforcement Task Force on the occasion of their twentieth-anniversary conference on July 30, 2002, Attorney General John Ashcroft told the audience, "Law enforcement has been aware for some time of significant linkages between terrorism and drug trafficking."[1] If that's true, we're not getting much bang for our buck out of whoever's supposed to be spreading the news, because every law-enforcement and drug agency in the country has missed the Arab–East African drug-smuggling network operating in America, bringing hundreds of tons of an illegal narcotic worth billions of dollars annually into this country—and using the profits to fund terrorism.

Most Americans have never heard of the drug that is the currency of this terrorism network. It goes by different names in different places. In Yemen, it's *qat*; it's *tschat* in Ethiopia; and in

Kenya it's *miraa*. On the streets of America it's called khat, and although to possess or distribute khat in America is a crime, its sale and distribution are on the rise in every corner of our nation.

Our ignorance is the result of the government's failure to launch a national investigation into the link between terrorism and khat smuggling, despite the huge quantity of it seized annually by the Customs Service and DEA briefs that state the facts clearly. It's bad enough most Americans are unaware of khat—that's why most police and local law officials never heard of it, either. Put khat on dinner plates at a banquet for any national law-enforcement organization in the country and the narcotic would draw less attention than a healthy portion of green leafy vegetables.

"At first, I couldn't figure out why so much 'rhubarb' was in the car," reported a West Virginia State Trooper who found it during a routine stop. A Merriam Police Department officer in Kansas City, Kansas, just thought the hundred pounds of khat in the trunk of a car he stopped was "a huge salad."[2]

Khat is the fresh leaves, twigs, and stalks of the evergreen shrub *Catha edulis*. It grows twenty-feet high in the dry soil of East Africa and the Arabian Peninsula (see the appendix). Dried, khat can be boiled into tea, smoked, and even sprinkled on food. Other street names for it are *Abyssinian tea, African salad, oat, kat, chat,* and *catha*. Khat sellers often put ads on signs in ethnic restaurants, bars, grocery stores, and smoke shops catering to Arabs.

Khat is a narcotic. Its psychoactive ingredient, cathinone, is listed in Schedule I of the Controlled Substances Act, the most restrictive category used by the Drug Enforcement Administration (DEA). Yet a Street Advisory from the New York Office of Alcoholism and Substance Abuse Services from as far back as 1993 warns, "Khat is becoming increasingly available in the US, especially in cities like NY, DC, LA, Boston, Dallas, and Detroit."[3] The cost of khat has risen, too, from about $30 to $60 per kilogram in 1992 to $400 to $500 per kilogram in 2003. It is sold on the street as a bundle of about forty twigs for $50; twenty bundles per kilogram.

Driving up the price is the sharp increase in immigrants from Somalia, Ethiopia, and Yemen who continue to use khat in the United States. "If you are in a community with Somalian immigrants, khat is coming," said Minnesota State Patrolman Lieutenant Doug Thooft in a report done by the American Prosecutors Research Institute, a research bureau for district attorneys.[4] Reflecting that trend, U.S. Customs seized 3.6 tons of khat during Ramadan alone—November 6 through December 5, 2002—an increase the DEA says is linked to khat's ability to reduce fatigue and appetite, and Islam's requirement that Muslims fast during Ramadan, their most important religious holiday of the year.

Muslim males chew khat at social gatherings, a cultural tradition older than drinking coffee in some regions. The thick wad of chewed leaves, called a *quid,* is kept between cheek and gum. Chewing it releases the cathinone whose amphetamine-like effect alleviates fatigue and reduces appetite. One immigrant described it as "like what you would get from two or three beers—that little feeling that lets people forget problems and troubles. It makes talking and communicating a lot more easier somehow. You feel like you are suddenly very, very alert."[5]

The truth is that the use of khat among Muslim immigrants is as socially and morally damaging as alcohol has been to Native Americans, or crack cocaine to the inhabitants of our inner cities. Common side effects of continued khat use include anorexia, heart disease, hypertension, insomnia, gastric disorders, and the kind of blackened teeth seen in the film *Black Hawk Down.*

Several million people worldwide currently use khat. Khat is grown in export quantities in Kenya and Ethiopia. It's Ethiopia's fourth-largest export, according to the U.S. embassy. A staggering 33 percent or more of Yemen's gross national product is associated with the cultivation, consumption, and export of khat. Somalia has 6 million people, a GNP of roughly $2 billion, and the average annual per capita income is less than $400. Khat spending totals $300,000 a day—over $100 million annually, bleeding the country dry.

The huge profits from selling khat make the terror network ignore the fact that chronic use can also produce physical exhaustion, violence, hyperactivity, hallucinations, psychosis, and suicidal depression. Maryam Warsame, leader of the Somali Women's Association in Columbus, says khat is to blame for the breakup of many marriages. Men go off to use khat, and "it is the woman who has to stay with the children, take care of the house. Sometimes the paycheck does not come home. They have to pay whoever is selling the khat, instead of giving it to their family, to their children."[6]

U.S. Customs has a rule of thumb that the annual amount of any controlled substance it confiscates trying to cross our borders represents less than ten percent of the total substance that actually crosses them. In 2001, Customs seized forty tons of khat, more than doubling the figure from five years earlier. A year later, Customs interdicted over seventy tons. That means a whopping *seven hundred tons* of khat plant were chewed, smoked, boiled, and brewed all over America.

Using the 2002 number for khat seizures reported by the DEA and the National Drug Intelligence Center (NDIC), and averaging the cost of khat in New York the same year, seven hundred tons of khat has a street value of more than $1.5 *billion*. No one, not even the most unaware or uninformed, would relegate a drug worth a billion and half dollars to unimportance or ignore the need for an urgent investigation into the money's ultimate destination.

A comparison that helps appreciate the extent of khat smuggling in this country: The statistics in the Federal-wide Drug Seizure System (FDSS) show that U.S. federal authorities seized "only" 107 metric tons of cocaine in 2000, and 111 metric tons in 2001. At that rate, all things being equal, consumption of cocaine and khat in America will equalize within a few short years.

Khat flows into America in a continuous stream. Every day from January 2002 to September 2002, Customs officers seized khat in packages coming into the delivery facility in Memphis International Airport. Sources in the Customs Service also reported a dramatic rise in khat seizures at JFK and at Miami International Airport after 9/11. One Customs officer who works out "on the line" speculated to me that the increase might simply be due to the heightened surveillance on everything coming from that region of the world—khat might always have been coming into America at that rate.

According to Shaker al-Ashwal's article "Qat in America," New York is the base for the distribution of khat. Khat loses its potency quickly, so it is generally shipped to the United States on Thursdays, Fridays, and Saturdays for weekend use, according to khat sellers in New York.[7] The cathinone in the fresh leaves breaks down within forty-eight hours, unless refrigerated. To get khat to its intended market quickly, it is primarily transported from Great Britain to the United States via package delivery services or couriers aboard commercial aircraft. When shipped by package delivery services it is usually listed on manifests as Abyssinian or African tea, African salad, molokheya—an Egyptian vegetable—tobacco leaves, perishable lettuce or fresh vegetables, and herbs. It was listed as auto parts on at least one occasion.

In a speech to the Organized Crime and Drug Enforcement Task Force, the attorney general told the audience, "Earlier this year, I asked federal law-enforcement agencies to identify for the first time on a single list the major trafficking organizations that are responsible for the U.S. drug supply."

Whoever compiled the list forgot khat.

Khat is yet another case of federal agencies not putting the pieces of the puzzle together. The DEA is certainly aware of the connection between drugs and terrorism, according to its 2002 Drug Intelligence brief, "Drugs and Terrorism: A New Perspective":

> Prior to September 11, 2001, drug trafficking and terrorist activities were usually addressed by the law enforcement community as separate issues. In the wake of the terrorist attacks in New York City, Washington, DC, and Pennsylvania, the public now perceives these two criminal activities as intertwined. For the Drug Enforcement Administration investigating the link between drugs and terrorism has taken on renewed importance.
>
> Criminals, by exploiting advances in technology, finance, communications, and transportation in pursuit of their illegal endeavors, have become criminal entrepreneurs. Perhaps the most alarming aspect of this "entrepreneurial" style of crime is the intricate manner in which drugs and terrorism may be intermingled. Since September 11th, the public's image of terrorism is magnified. Not only is the proliferation of illegal drugs perceived as a danger, but also the proceeds from drugs are among the sources for funding for other criminal activities, including terrorism.

That DEA Intelligence Brief and another released on June 2002 make it appear that the DEA knows about khat. The June 2002 brief describes almost every aspect of khat and states point-blank in the first paragraph: "Individuals of East African and Middle Eastern descent are most often responsible for the importation, distribution, possession, and use of khat in the United States." The entire Intelligence Brief can be viewed online at http://www.usdoj.gov/dea/pubs/intel/02032/02032p.html.

The National Drug Intelligence Center of the U.S. Department of Justice is the primary center for strategic domestic counter-drug intelligence, and it, too, has a mass of reports on khat. Interestingly, the NDIC report shows that despite the government's lack of interest, some local police departments are doing their job:

• In Hennepin County, which includes the Minneapolis area, khat-related charges have been filed against 10 to 20 people in the past year (2002), said Dan Rogan, spokesman for the county attorney's office. St. Paul–Minneapolis has the nation's largest Somali community, estimated at fifty thousand members.[8]

• In Columbus, Ohio, Sgt. Ben Casuccio said that police confiscated 9 pounds of khat in 2000. In 2001 Columbus police seized 633 pounds. Thus far, police have seized 860 pounds of khat this year (2002).[9]

• In Minneapolis–St. Paul, Minnesota: On December 31, 2002, USCS officials seized over 146 kilograms of khat concealed in seven boxes shipped from the United Kingdom and arrested a 29-year-old Minneapolis resident as he accepted receipt of the boxes.[10]

• In New York, New York: In August 2002 USCS officials seized 22 packages containing more than 59 kilograms of khat that had arrived in New York from London. The packages were addressed to individuals in several U.S. cities. During a subsequent controlled delivery, the Kansas City, Kansas, Police Department Interdiction Unit arrested four male Somali nationals and one male Ethiopian national. The Omaha Commercial Interdiction Unit also conducted a controlled delivery and arrested two Somali nationals.[11]

• In Kansas City, Missouri: In March 2002 USCS officials seized over 68 kilograms of khat concealed in five boxes shipped from London and arrested two Somali nationals who accepted receipt of the boxes in Kansas City.[12]

• In Kansas City, Kansas: On October 2002, officers of the Merriam Police Department arrested two Somali men from Minneapolis who were attempting to retrieve several packages containing khat that had been shipped from London, England, to various locations throughout the Kansas City area.[13]

• In Detroit, Michigan: On January 13, 2003, USCS officials seized almost 80 kilograms of khat concealed in the luggage of two British women arriving from London. Law-enforcement officials executed a controlled delivery of the khat to a hotel near the airport and arrested two Somali men from Nashville, Tennessee, who attempted to receive the drug. The two Somali men were to transport the khat by private vehicle back to Tennessee for distribution among the Somali community in Nashville.[14]

• Controlled deliveries have also been made in Minneapolis, Norfolk, Seattle, and Sioux City.

There seems no doubt that the khat-distribution network is run by Somali and Yemeni immigrants. To follow up the investigations, I spoke with Sergeant Michael Daniels of the Merriam Police Department in Kansas City, Kansas, on March 25, 2004. He confirmed the NDIC report that his officers had arrested two Somali men from Minneapolis attempting to retrieve several packages containing khat. The packages had been shipped from London, England, to various locations throughout the Kansas area. The packages were addressed to various individuals with Middle Eastern names and delivered to ten different hotels via package-delivery services. The khat was to be distributed in Minneapolis. At the time of their arrest, the men had retrieved seven of the packages; the police collected the other three.

Sergeant Daniels stated that the Somalis admitted that they had brought in the khat before and thought it to be legal. But when the police inquired, "If you thought it was legal, why didn't you have it delivered to your home?" The Somali's ability to speak English took a sharp downturn. It appeared to the officers that the Somalis were not "big players," but a lawyer flew in from Atlanta, Georgia, to defend them. It seemed "as if this lawyer just filled in the blanks of a standard defense that he had already successfully completed elsewhere." Considering the out-of-state attorney, the cash, drugs, and other evidence establishing probable cause that cannot be printed here, the police called in the FBI. To date, the Merriam Police Department has never been informed by the FBI of the outcome of its investigation, or if the FBI has even conducted one.

I spoke to Sergeant Ben Cassuccio of the Columbus, Ohio, Police Department. Columbus has a Somali population of ap-

proximately thirty thousand, the second-largest Somali con-
centration in the United States. Sergeant Cassuccio told me he
first started to notice khat in his community between 1999 and
2000, and that most of the khat was wrapped in British newspapers.

Sergeant Cassuccio has also worked on some controlled
buys. They showed that the money trail, through a money-
laundering scheme, led to Yemen. Our State Department's figures show almost one-third of Yemen's GNP is related to khat.
Yemen is also a nation listed as one that supports terrorism.

The sergeant has traveled across the country trying to get
law-enforcement agencies and district attorneys interested in
aggressively prosecuting khat offenders but with no takers. In
fact, his cases are among the few in the country to obtain convictions. He has also lobbied aggressively for the UK to make
khat illegal to eliminate London as a central point of distribution, again with little result for his efforts.

The sad conclusion is that most federal prosecutors won't
prosecute khat cases because they are not as "sexy" as cocaine
and heroin busts, but it is also a case of political correctness
ruling the day more. Going after khat would center on Middle
Eastern immigrants and their communities, and many police
officers have told me in private that the resulting antagonism
and lawsuits from civil liberties extremists simply cost too
much time and money to fight.

They have good reason to feel this way.

Immigrant's rights groups like the Somali Justice Advocacy
Center in St. Paul say that their people are being targeted, and

these people are unaware they are breaking the law. Police say immigrants know khat has been illegal in the United States since 1993.

Omar Jamal, executive manager of the Somali Justice Advocacy Center, insists, "What coffee is to Americans is what khat is for Somalis. The whole thing about khat being addictive is very strange for Somalis. It's a completely different frame of thinking."[15]

Jamal also said Minneapolis police have pulled over young Somalis in search of khat, which he considers racial profiling. DEA spokesman David Jacobson in Detroit said no ethnic community is targeted.

Although Jamal is not linked to it, the Islamic terror network also tries to obscure both the cost and the danger of khat, claiming racial prejudice is behind the police enforcing the law. Charges that arrests are minority-bashing make it far more difficult to expose khat's presence in America. Disputes about khat's potency or social history just camouflage the drug network that smuggles it.

Khat is as dangerous as any other controlled substance, most of which have been linked to funding terrorism. We need a congressional investigation that will establish once and for all the facts about the import and distribution network of khat, and the link between khat-derived profits and the murder of American citizens

It's unusual for Great Britain to be the cause of problems in the United States, but the fact is that U.S. Customs officers at

New York's JFK International Airport make most of their khat seizures from packages arriving overnight by express mail, or passengers coming from London. Despite the fact that khat is illegal in most of Europe, it is legal in Great Britain, where it is consumed by a very large Somali community. Estimates are that 90 percent of Somali men reportedly chew the leaves regularly.

The BBC reports that "highly organised gangs in Britain are making £150 million a year smuggling Khat into the U.S."[16] These gangs have also been linked to murder. The British criminal syndicates ship khat from London by FedEx and other air couriers within hours of its arrival. They also recruit young local British men to act as "mules," to carry it hidden in their luggage. For a plane ticket and a few pounds, mules fly to the United States carrying khat in their suitcases. DEA reports indicate that of the twenty-seven metric tons seized by Customs in 1998, almost eighteen metric tons were seized from passengers arriving from Great Britain. The traffic is heaviest near the weekend, when demand is highest, and in 2003, more than twenty Brits were arrested in this country attempting to smuggle in khat.

In October 2003, *BBC ONE South East* broadcast this report:

This spring, US enforcement officers were surprised to find 12 young, white males—all from the town of Deal—locked up in New York's notorious Rikers Island jail. One of them, 17-year-old David McGahan, was targeted in a pub and offered £500 to take a couple of suitcases over to America. His parents thought he was at a party in Dover when they got the call. His mother, Majorie, recalls: "We had no idea he had left the country even. He said 'Mum, I'm really sorry. I didn't realize I'd get myself into so much trouble.' He was in tears."

Legal in Britain, it can be bought in certain green grocers and markets for about £5 a bunch—but it can command high sums of money in America. Banned in most countries, including mainland Europe, it is legally imported into the UK where the smugglers dupe people into acting as couriers.[17]

Almost all the cases of British kids caught at JFK smuggling khat have been assigned to a pert, articulate Queens County Legal Aide defense attorney named Elizabeth Prusser. Her office gets all the drug-smuggling cases because JFK International Airport is in Queens. She has become an expert in drug cases, including cocaine, heroin, and other substances. Ms. Prusser also defended almost all the British kids caught smuggling khat. It is unimportant to Ms. Prusser that her clients are often without resources. She fights like a mother tiger protecting her young.

I had the pleasure of speaking with Ms. Prusser in April 2004, and she told me what the British youths caught smuggling khat all told her: They were initially recruited in a local bar by other British youths who offered them £500 in cash and a free trip to New York if they would agree to bring some packages with them. If the kid said okay, they were sent to London and put up overnight in a hotel. In the morning they were met by two or three men they described as dark-complexioned Arabs who gave them their plane tickets and suitcases filled with khat. They were given the name of a hotel near the airport and instructions to go there after clearing Customs. They would be met by someone when they arrived.

Only one of Ms. Prusser's khat cases involved someone other than a British national—a Somali man who was told to go to the JFK Inn on South Conduit Avenue in Queens. He was also told that someone would meet him. Like the British kids, he never got there to complete the connection.

With khat legal in the UK, a case could be made that all of them might not have known they were breaking the law. No one is that stupid. If taking the suitcases was on the up and up, why would the Arabs go to the trouble of recruiting and paying someone else to do it? No, like all kids, they did it because they didn't think they would be caught. Like all kids, it was a rude awakening when they were.

I finally understood how the U.S. attorney and other federal agencies could avoid prosecuting khat cases, when Ms. Prusser spoke about the laws that governed them. First, there is no Probable Cause at borders. Customs can search anyone for any reason. Second, a ticket paid for in cash is one of the sure signs of a mule. So is making frequent trips of short duration to the same destination. Third, there is dual jurisdiction at JFK—federal and state.

When U.S. Customs picks up a drug courier, federal agents grill the person for hours. Like the British youths, most have little to tell. They can't identify the Arabs who gave them the khat, they don't know who they were going to meet in New York, and the tickets were paid for in cash so there's no way to trace the Arabs who bought them.

Federal agents must then decide either to have the U.S. attorney's office file federal charges or "kick" the courier to state jurisdiction and have the New York City Police Department arrest the courier. Prosecuting a khat case is very difficult. Khat has two psychoactive chemicals: cathinone, a Schedule 1 substance, and cathine, a Schedule IV substance. Unless the fresh leaves are refrigerated, the cathinone will break down within forty-eight hours, leaving only cathine.

Khat needs priority testing in police and FBI drug labs very soon after it's seized. Customs and U.S. attorneys would rather prosecute a high-profile cocaine or heroin smuggler, cases that might make the news. Khat cases are assigned so little importance, it is rarely tested at all. Defense attorneys are sometimes able to get their clients off because the cathinone is virtually absent by the time the khat evidence is analyzed.

Federal agents also kick drug couriers over to the state because New York's Rockefeller Drug Laws are actually harsher than federal statutes. In New York State, khat smuggling is an A-1 felony, the same category as murder. The courier faces a minimum of fifteen years to life imprisonment. For this reason, the preferred mule is under fifteen—still a juvenile.

As a defense attorney, Ms. Prusser has few options other than "begging and pleading" to lessen the sentence. She can't go to trial and win—the kids were caught in the act, their rights were not violated, and ignorance is not an excuse. Ms. Prusser speculated that her clients might have been "ratted out" by their Arab employers to keep Customs busy, enabling other couriers on the same plane to slip through unnoticed.

The more I looked into khat smuggling, the more difficult it was to figure out why no one was sounding the alarm. In December 2001, right after 9/11, the DEA formed a Special Coordination Unit at its Special Operations Division to coordinate DEA intelligence and investigations linked to terrorism. This was reported in a September 2002 brief:

> Terrorist organizations use a number of sources to garner funds for their activities, such as petty crimes, kidnap-for-ransom, charities, sympathizers, front companies, and drug trafficking. . . .
>
> [S]ome terrorist groups may be involved in all aspects of the drug trade, from cultivation, production, transportation, and wholesale distribution to money laundering. . . . No matter which form it takes . . . many terrorist groups are using drug money to fund their activities and perpetrate violence against governments and people around the world.[18]

Officially, that sounds just fine. However, when I asked the chief of operations of a major police department on Long Island in March 2004 about investigating khat and a link to terrorism, he told me his narcotics unit needed more information to be effective. Every police officer I spoke to who had any involvement with khat said there is reason to believe khat is supplying criminal enterprises involved with terrorism, and that it has to be investigated aggressively. Many believe that khat will soon reach other groups besides Middle Easterners.

One summed it up this way: "When they find out that forty dollars buys three days of high, why use crack?"

In February of 2004, I asked a supervisor of the Highway Patrol in New York State to test law enforcement's level of awareness of khat. The supervisor was eager to learn if anyone else was investigating khat, lest it turn into the same kind of national nightmare he had worked with as an undercover narcotics officer in 1976: he saw crack cocaine long before its use became epidemic, but his superiors weren't interested in investigating it. The supervisor sent a classified Internet query to law-enforcement personnel and officials involved in transportation safety. These are the responses.

From the Metropolitan Transportation Authority:

"An officer from the New York–New Jersey Port Authority told me his agency, in conjunction with Customs, made several khat arrests early last year but to his knowledge not any in recent memory."

"I posed the question of familiarity of khat on an informal group e-mail at work. So far, 3—No, 2—Yes. I have noticed an increase in the use of khat in the upstate NY area. This is probably due to the return of the drug from Somalia by military personnel who returned to the Fort Drum and surrounding areas, were introduced to khat and seek to continue the use of it."

From the New York State Department of Environmental Conservation:

"I have never heard of this drug."

"re KHAT—never heard of it."

From the New York State Department of Transportation:

MCI Supervising Investigator: "I have never heard of it here in the USA. Learned of it from *Black Hawk Down.*"

From Southern Chautaugua County, New York, Sheriff's Department:

"About three to four years ago I made a small seizure of khat on a vehicle stop. I had to call the DEA because I was not aware of it."

From the New York City Police Department:

"I have heard of khat and its fake manmade twin cat but have never seen either. Nor have I ever heard of enforcement or interdiction activities in the New York City area related to these items."

From the Shelter Island, New York, Police Department:

"Learned of it from PBS and History Channel specials on Mogadishu."

From the Centre Island, New York, Police Department:

"Never heard of khat."

Right now, khat use is confined to Muslim communities, but we can look to history to see what will most assuredly happen. America initially ignored crack cocaine, believing it was limited to the inner cities. It spread all over the country overnight, and our War on Drugs hasn't done anything about it except fill our prisons with offenders. Khat will spread, too, unless we stop it flowing into Muslim communities and prevent its profits from being used by militant Islam to wage their Holy War against us.

Khat and the Holy War on our home front are more dots federal authorities have failed to connect since 9/11. America is going to remain unsafe as long as our government fails to investigate the link between khat profits and terrorism. Nothing is more terrifying than the specter of Militant Islam and its secret network someday having sufficient wealth to adopt the model of organized crime: impervious to prosecution, protected by influence, wielding political power sufficient to reach its prime objective—our destruction.

CHAPTER 6

COUNTERFEITING RINGS

America's insatiable appetite for illicit drugs and knockoff designer items makes for an extraordinarily lucrative market. Trafficking in these commodities is a multibillion-dollar business. The cash raised is easy to dispose of with no discernible paper trail. Even drug-counterfeiting rings operate as cash enterprises. They don't maintain clear records and are quick to destroy any evidence and switch their location when detected.

The profits from these clandestine counterfeit operations are huge and often without much risk of capture and prosecution. Any enterprising terrorist conspiracy quickly understands how much money is at stake and steps up to the plate to fund its agenda. Whether it is a 100 percent profit from the street sale of a kilo of cocaine or a 900 percent profit through the resale of pirated software, there is much money to be made, often with little risk.[1]

It once seemed unlikely criminal activity could be linked to the prompt towing of abandoned vehicles or the quick removal of graffiti. Yet the "Broken Windows" theory of criminologists James Q. Wilson and George Kelling argued that disorder in a community, if left uncorrected, undercut residents' own efforts to maintain their homes and neighborhoods and to control unruly behavior. "When law-abiding eyes stop watching the streets, the social order breaks down and criminals move in."[2]

When law enforcement applied it to policing local neighborhoods, the theory worked. Scrupulously enforcing petty offenses like public drinking, turnstile jumping, and graffiti brought a decrease in more serious crimes like armed robbery and drug dealing.

"Broken Bottles" adapts Wilson and Kelling's successful crime-fighting strategy to the War on Terror. What appears to be a harmless knockoff designer item or an Internet Website hawking cheap prescription drugs might just be the tip of a terrorist iceberg. Unearthing these criminal activities and the entrepreneurs sustaining the terrorist operation is the best way to catch terrorists and to break the cycle of Jihadist violence. In this case, "Don't sweat the small stuff" is very bad advice.

"It wasn't until after September 11 that we understood the magnitude of the [terrorist] fund-raising from our own shores," said John Forbes, a former U.S. Customs official who directed a financial-crimes task force in New York. "We were always looking to catch the big rats in terror financing, but in looking for rats . . . thousands of ants got by."[3]

The importance of "Broken Bottles"—a reference to the mil-

lions of bottles of consumer products, from gray-market per-
fumes to counterfeit pharmaceuticals, flooding this country—is
connecting the right crimes to the desired results; that is, ex-
posing terrorists. A growing body of evidence indicates that terrorist organizations are already involved in, and profiting from,
large-scale intellectual-property theft, counterfeiting, and piracy,
and the following examples establish the connection:

• When Danish Customs examined one of the shipping containers in a delivery of goods from Dubai to Copenhagen, they
discovered it contained over one thousand crates full of counterfeit shampoos, creams, cologne, and perfume. The goods
were ultimately bound for the United Kingdom, which later revealed the sender of the counterfeit goods was a member of al
Qaeda, a connection confirmed by the European Commission's
Customs Coordination Office.[4]

• A raid of a souvenir shop in mid-town Manhattan found a
suitcase full of counterfeit watches containing flight manuals
for Boeing 767s, some containing handwritten notes in Arabic.[5]

• A raid on a counterfeit handbag shop in New York uncovered faxes relating to the purchase of bridge-inspection equipment.[6]

• Two weeks after the raid on the handbag shop, New Jersey
police investigating an assault on a Lebanese member of an organized crime syndicate found fake driver's licenses and lists of
suspected al Qaeda terrorists in the man's apartment—including the names of workers from the handbag shop that had been
raided.[7]

• Police also found al Qaeda terrorist-training manuals recommending the sale of fake goods as one means to raise funds to support terrorist operations.[8]

• Mohamad Hammoud was convicted in February 2003 and sentenced to 155 years in prison for leading a multimillion-dollar cigarette smuggling operation out of North Carolina that funneled money to Hezbollah.[9] The Hezbollah cell operated out of Charlotte, and over the course of a year and a half sold close to $8 million worth of smuggled cigarettes in the state of Michigan.[10] Ten members of the smuggling ring were arrested. Eight members pled guilty. And in June 2002, Hammoud was convicted of providing aid to a terrorist organization.[11] The indictment papers surrounding the case stated that Hezbollah officials in Lebanon asked cell members to purchase equipment such as "computers, night-vision equipment, mine-detection devices, global-positioning devices, and advanced aircraft-analysis software."[12]

In the early 1980s, the Lebanese terror organization Hezbollah issued a fatwa sanctioning drug trafficking as a means of killing Satan America and the Jews. The fatwa made it perfectly clear that if it was not possible to kill the infidels with guns, then it would permissible to use illicit drugs. The puritanical Taliban that nurtured Osama bin Laden's al Qaeda terrorists implemented a similar strategy when it allowed opium sales consumed by *kafirs,* unbelievers, in the West to fund its terror regime.

The State Department identified thirty-seven foreign terrorist organizations in its "Patterns of Global Terrorism 2003," plus a list of forty other terrorist groups the report identifies as active in the past year, not included here. Designation of a group as a foreign terrorist organization results in the U.S. government blocking assets held in U.S. financial institutions, denying their members visas, and making it a criminal offense for U.S. citizens or persons within U.S. jurisdiction to provide them with material support or resources.

Designated Foreign Terrorist Organizations

Abu Nidal Organization (ANO)

Abu Sayyaf Group (ASG)

Al-Aqsa Martyrs Brigade

Amal

Ansar al-Islam (AI)

Armed Islamic Group (GIA)

'Asbat al-Ansar

Aum Supreme Truth (Aum) Aum Shinrikyo, Aleph

Basque Fatherland and Liberty (ETA)

Communist Party of Philippines/New People's Army
  (CPP/NPA)

Al-Gama'a al-Islamiyya (Islamic Group, IG)

Hamas (Islamic Resistance Movement)

Harakat ul Mujahideen (HUM)

Hezbollah (Party of God)

Islamic Movement of Uzbekistan (IMU)

Jaish-e-Mohammed (JEM)

Jemaah Islamiya (JI)

Al-Jihad (Egyptian Islamic Jihad, EIJ)

Kahane Chai (Kach)

Kongra-Gel (KGK, formerly Kurdistan Workers' Party, PKK,
 KADEK)
Lashkar-e-Tayyiba (LT)
Lashkar I Jhangvi (LJ)
Liberation Tigers of Tamil Eelam (LTTE)
Mujahideen-e Khalq Organization (MEK or MKO)
National Liberation Army (ELN), Colombia
Palestinian Islamic Jihad (PIJ)
Palestine Liberation Front (PLF)
Popular Front for the Liberation of Palestine (PFLP)
Popular Front for the Liberation of Palestine-General
 Command (PFLP-GC)
Al Qaeda
Real IRA (RIRA)
Revolutionary Armed Forces of Colombia (FARC)
Revolutionary Nuclei (RN)
Revolutionary Organization 17 November (17 November)
Revolutionary People's Liberation Party/Front (DHKP/C) 135
Salafist Group for Call and Combat (GSPC)
Sendero Luminoso (Shining Path or SL)
United Self-Defense Forces/Group of Colombia (AUC)

In order to survive, these terrorist organizations develop and maintain reliable and low-key sources of funding. Behind the suicide bombers, hijackers, and gunmen stand "criminal entrepreneurs and financiers in suits who understand the best way to bankroll Armageddon is through the capitalist system."[13]

Terrorist organizations are attracted to counterfeiting and

piracy because they are lucrative businesses, but also because they allow terrorists to remain relatively anonymous. Counterfeiting and piracy rings often operate as cash enterprises, they lease manufacturing equipment from third parties, and generally do not maintain reliable paperwork or business records. Upon suspicion of detection, terrorist counterfeiters can move merchandise, hide assets and equipment, switch manufacturing locations, destroy evidence, or simply disappear without leaving a paper trail. And, most important, any profits made in this type of underground market are obviously difficult to trace.

The amount of money that can be raised from counterfeiting and piracy is staggering. A recent article in *Time* magazine analyzed the issue of software piracy and offered the following scenario: for an outlay of $47,000—and a lot less risk than dealing drugs like cocaine or heroin—an enterprising crook can buy fifteen hundred pirated copies of Office 2000 Pro and resell them for between $150,000 to $300,000.

In February 2003, federal prosecutors in Brooklyn, New York, charged six men with importing up to 35 million counterfeit cigarettes from China into the United States. The men were accused of importing the fake cigarettes, then selling them through a tax-free business located at an upstate New York Indian reservation and also through the Web site www.smokecheap.com.

The cigarettes were allegedly imported into the United States in five separate shipments through New Jersey ports over a two-year period. The charging documents stated that the counterfeiters hid the cigarettes in shipping containers behind kitchen pots. According to the prosecutors, the men were under investigation in Europe for cigarette smuggling. "Two of the defendants were also charged with importing counterfeit batteries from China via Lithuania.[14] The profits from a criminal operation of this scope and nature, if successful, could easily have stretched into the millions of dollars."

In 1996, the FBI confiscated 100,000 counterfeit T-shirts bearing fake and unauthorized Nike "swoosh" or Olympic logos that were intended to be sold at the 1996 Summer Olympic Games. "The operation generated millions of dollars and was run by the followers of Sheik Omar Abdel-Rahman, the blind cleric who was later sentenced to 240 years in prison for plotting to bomb New York City landmarks.[15]

"The pharmaceutical market provides similar opportunities to make significant money through the sale of bogus and potentially lethal drugs and medications. A 2001 investigation in the state of Florida revealed that a criminal ring had counterfeited Procrit, a drug used to improve the immune systems of cancer and HIV patients. The ring members relabeled about 110,000 bottles of the drug Epogen to give the appearance that they contained dosages of Procrit, a drug twenty times stronger than Epogen. The counterfeiters then moved the fake drugs into the market through four separate wholesalers. Investigators discovered some of the drugs in Texas and North Carolina, but ultimately recovered only 10 percent of the 110,000 counterfeit bottles. The Florida Bureau of Statewide Pharmaceutical Services estimated the counterfeiter's profit to be $46 million."[16]

The Procrit counterfeiters are not alone. Since 1996 the Federal Drug Administration has diligently investigated seventy-one counterfeit drug cases, resulting in twenty-six convictions.[17] "These numbers become even more alarming when one considers the fact that the September 11 attacks cost only $500,000— a little more than $26,000 per terrorist—certainly not a large or unattainable amount of money."[18] Based on the above figures, just one single successful large-scale intellectual-property crime could potentially fund multiple terrorist attacks.

Although the U.S. drug supply is still considered the safest in the world, it can be easily compromised to be used not only to finance a terrorist attack, it can be used to mount one.

I had a conversation sometime before 9/11 with an Egyptian pharmacist visiting this country who told me how much cheaper it was to manufacture pharmaceuticals in the Middle East. He showed me an Egyptian version of an antibiotic he traveled with for a persistent nasal infection. He manufactured the antibiotic and knew everything about all phases of production.

I was amazed at its similarity to the drug prescribed for me by my allergist to treat a similar condition. In fact, I had to examine it closely to gauge the difference, and it was not until I saw the package it came in that I was able to tell. A slight modification in the packaging and the antibiotic could pass off as the real deal. The unsuspecting consumer or wholesaler would be none the wiser.

The possibility of a terrorist using that similarity is too strong to ignore. The following anecdotal accounts illustrate the extent of the health and safety risks presented by the sale of counterfeit goods; as well as the alarming range of methods through which terrorists could launch a deadly attack against the United States:

• The World Health Organization (WHO) estimates that counterfeit drugs account for 10 percent of all pharmaceuticals. That number can rise to as high as 60 percent in developing countries.[19] "According to the WHO, 16% of counterfeit drugs contain the wrong ingredients, 17% contain incorrect amounts of the proper ingredients, and 60% have no active ingredients whatsoever."[20]

• "In New York, a sixteen-year-old liver-transplant recipient received eight weeks worth of injections of counterfeit Epogen to treat his anemia and to raise his red blood cell count. The treatments, instead of improving the boy's condition, caused excruciating aches and spasms. The vials used for the injections were supposed to contain 40,000 units of the drug; instead, the counterfeit version contained only 2,000 units. Other counterfeit lots of Epogen were also found in Texas."[21]

• "In 2002 a New York County district attorney charged seven people and five companies in the United States, China, and India with selling counterfeit Viagra over the Internet. Undercover officers purchased over 25,000 pills. Some pills were smuggled into the United States in stereo speakers and stuffed toys. One supplier told the agents that he could supply 2.5 million tablets a month."[22]

• On June 7, 2001, the chief of security for the drug company Novartis International AG testified before a House Subcommittee that one counterfeit ring produced "millions of yellow tablets that were virtually indistinguishable from the genuine product." The fake tablets were "made of boric acid, floor wax, and lead-based yellow paint used for road markings."[23]

In recent months, Democratic lawmakers have been urging a governmental task force chaired by Surgeon General Richard Carmona to allow the import of cheaper drugs from Canada. A Minnesota seniors group has slapped nine pharmaceutical manufacturers with a lawsuit in U.S. District Court in Minneapolis. The lawsuit alleges that these drugmakers have conspired to keep U.S. medicine prices artificially high by blocking Canadian imports.[24]

While Canadian imports might help out cash-strapped seniors or anyone else on a strict budget, they raise serious safety issues that go well beyond matters of quality control. Adding to these safety issues is the growing use of the Internet to lure prescription-drug buyers with promises of lower prices.

William K. Hubbard, associate commissioner for Policy and Planning at the Food and Drug Administration, addressed the Committee on Government Reform of the U.S. House of Representatives on Internet drug sales, pointing out that a number of drug Web sites "present risks to purchasers and unique challenges to regulators, law enforcement officials and policy makers."[25]

The challenges to law-enforcement officials involve mail fraud, money laundering, and related crimes. "In 2002 Mohamad Mostafa was convicted for being part of a conspiracy to sell counterfeit infant formula. Mohamad Mostafa was also in the country illegally and upon indictment in 1995 fled to Canada, where he was finally arrested in 2001."[26]

The potential harm that could be done by terrorists substituting counterfeit pharmaceuticals that, in place of the proper ingredients, actually contain deadly chemicals, poisons, or biological toxins is beyond measure. It would certainly not be difficult for terrorists to insert such deadly products into the stream of commerce. This is especially true in a time where an increasing number of pharmaceuticals are coming from sources that are often beyond the reach of regulators at both the federal and state levels. Frighteningly, this analysis covers only the pharmaceutical industry. The harm that could be inflicted via intellectual property–related crimes simply cannot be ignored or dismissed.[27]

As with many other aspects of the post–9/11 world, even automobile parts, airplane parts, cosmetics, shampoos, and food items present risks:

• "A Norwegian plane crash in 1989 that killed 55 people resulted, in part, from substandard shear bolts and sleeves of an unknown origin."[28]

• The FAA estimates that 2 percent of the 26 million airline parts installed each year are counterfeit—roughly 520,000 parts.[29]

• "The operational life of counterfeit bearing-seal spacers removed from a United Airlines plane was found to be 600 hours—the genuine parts had an operational life of 20,000 hours—the fake parts came complete with fake boxes, labels, and paperwork, and were discovered only because of a vigilant airline mechanic. In another case, Delta Airlines discovered that an engine-mount cone-bolt (a device that actually fastens the engine to the planc) was counterfeit."[30]

• "In 1987 seven children died when the bus they were riding in flipped over. The brakes that were just installed on the bus bore a well-known trademark. Further examination, however, showed they were made of sawdust."[31]

• "In a federal case in California, the court determined the defendant sold counterfeit helicopter parts that caused several helicopters to crash, resulting in injuries and death."[32]

• "Counterfeit parts have been discovered in helicopters sold to NATO, in jet engines, bridge joints, and fasteners in areas of nuclear facilities responsible for preventing the meltdown of the reactor itself."[33]

• "In the mid-1990s a well-known shampoo producer was forced to place newspaper ads in over twenty-five papers to warn consumers about the presence of fake versions of its shampoo that contained unsafe levels of bacteria."[34]

• Fake toothpaste has also found its way into drugstores.[35]

One of the key missions of the Customs department in the past was the enforcement of intellectual-property rights at our borders, but as a consequence of the shift in Customs mission priorities, intellectual-property enforcement has been relegated to the sidelines. Some effects of the decrease in intellectual-property enforcement are already evident. The International

Anti-Counterfeiting Coalition in Washington, D.C., warns that intellectual-property theft is no longer a top enforcement concern for U.S. Customs.

The application of "Broken Bottles" can have what former secretary of Housing and Urban Development Henry G. Cisneros called a "signaling function."[36] In short, it is the ability to repel offenders when conditions change and the area is perceived as a less vulnerable and more risky site for crime. Lest we send a signal that terrorists are free to do business in the country, and to use that business to harm our citizens, "Broken Bottles" demands that we not only adamantly maintain but upgrade the investigation and prosecution of counterfeiting and intellectual-property theft to eliminate a source of funding and a potential means of attack for terrorism, and to arrest and bring to trial the terrorists living among us.

CHAPTER 7

MEDIA

On September 5, 2001, the North Texas Joint Terrorism Task Force, composed of agents from the FBI, the Secret Service, and the U.S. Customs Service, operating out of Dallas, executed a search warrant on the INFOCOM Corporation in Richardson, Texas, based on a two-year investigation into its ties to Hamas. The government froze INFOCOM bank accounts containing $70,000 of a $250,000 investment in the company made in 1993 by Nadia Elashi Marzook, the wife of Mousa Abu Marzook—a founding father of the secret Islamic network.[1] Marzook denied he had a connection to the military wing of Hamas, claiming his job was just raising funds for "political action initiatives" in the United States.

INFOCOM was owned by the Elashi brothers—Ghassan, Bayan, Basman, and Hazim. The company hosted close to five hundred Arabic Web sites, including Al-Jazeera television, and the newspaper *Al-Sharq*. It also sold computers and Internet services to Islamic organizations and businesses in the United States and the Middle East. A fifth brother, Ihsan Elashyi, worked at INFOCOM before founding the Tetrabal Corporation, which also sold and exported computers, software, and telecom equipment.

Ghassan Elashi was also the chairman of the Richardson–based Holy Land Foundation for Relief and Development.[2] INFOCOM serviced the HLF Website that raised money and recruited members. HLF was also the group Treasury Secretary Paul O'Neill said, "masquerades as a charity, while its primary purpose is to fund Hamas."[3]

Two years later, an August 2003 indictment charged that Abu Marzook conspired with INFOCOM and five of its employees to hide his financial transactions—to launder money. The indictment alleges that INFOCOM continued to engage in financial transactions with Abu Marzook after his designation as a terrorist, in violation of the International Emergency Economic Powers Act.[4] The agreement called for periodic payments to Nadia as a return on the investment. In 1995, when the United States designated Mousa Abu Marzook a Specially Designated Terrorist, it precluded others from having financial dealings with him. Nevertheless, the Elashi brothers continued to make payments to him by disguising them as payments to Nadia. All were charged with money laundering and violations of IEEPA.[5]

In addition, Abu Marzook, his wife, the five Elashi brothers, and INFOCOM were "charged with illegal exports, making false statements on export declarations, dealing in the property of a designated terrorist, conspiracy and money laundering. Ghassan Elashi and his brothers were charged with illegally selling computers and computer parts to Libya and Syria, both designated state sponsors of terrorism."[6]

U.S. Attorney General John Ashcroft detailed the link between INFOCOM and HLF, which also received financial backing from Abu Marzook, at a December 4, 2001, press conference: "The Holy Land Foundation for Relief and Development, based in Richardson, Texas, shares employees of an Internet company known as INFOCOM. . . . INFOCOM, like the Holy Land Foundation, received much of its early money from Mousa Abu Marzook, a top Hamas official who, the U.S. courts have determined, was directly involved in terrorism."[7]

Following a June 2002 guilty plea, Ihsan Elashyi was sentenced to forty-eight months' imprisonment and ordered to pay nearly $300,000 restitution and forfeit several properties, including a 2002 Chevrolet Tahoe, a 2001 BMW motorcycle, and three Rolex watches. Ghassan Elashi, Bayan Elashi, Basman Elashi, and Hazim Elashi were arrested in Dallas. Abu Marzook and his wife are living abroad.

The connections that define the secret Islamic terror network are clearly visible. Two high-ranking Hamas operatives arrested by the Israelis in January 1993 said Abu Marzook specifically directed funds toward Hamas's terror activities, encouraged acts of terror, and played an integral role in overseeing certain military aspects of Hamas's operations.

Abu Marzook raised money in America or abroad—the money was transferred to INFOCOM by his wife—INFO-COM laundered the money, paying Nadia, who passed the funds to Marzook, who directed the funds toward Hamas terror activities by contributing to HLF, which funded Hamas.

All the while, the media arm of the secret network was working hard to prevent exposure by using the automatic charge of racism, as well as outright lies, to obfuscate the issues. A statement from ten American Islamic organizations, including the Muslim Public Affairs Council, condemned the search as "an anti-Muslim witch hunt promoted by the pro-Israel lobby in America." Mahdi Bray, of the Los Angeles–based Muslim Public Affairs Council, held a news conference outside the closed INFOCOM office to make this statement: "We are deeply concerned that there is a pattern of stereotyping that permeates all these types of investigations. There is a marginalization of the American-Muslim population."[8]

After the 9/11 terrorist attacks, the government was somewhat more aggressive in trying to shut down Websites that provided material support for terrorism. It's a daunting task. Sites go up, they're closed down, they go up again somewhere else. The problem is even greater with sites originating outside this country as states such as Syria and Iran allow terrorists to operate freely on the Internet. Far more political pressure is needed, and a rigorous scientific inquiry into how best to locate and shut down these sites.

Muslim groups have long used the Internet to suggest violence in the name of Islam. Al-Muhajiroun, an extremist Muslim group headquartered at the Finsbury Park Mosque in north London, is such a group. The group's leader, Sheikh Omar Baki Muhammad, gained worldwide attention in 2002 when he announced a conference to celebrate "The Magnificent 19." He meant the 9/11 hijackers.

Al-Muhajiroun has a considerable following in the New York metropolitan area. On its Website, www.Muhajiroun.com, it notes: "There is no Copyright in Islam/Please feel free to copy and distribute any part of this website, however please do not change any of the content found in this website." The content is easy to understand—Islam must dominate the world through violent Jihad.

Another call to violence can be found on the Website of Maktab Al Jihad, www.maktab-al-jihad.com. This on-again-off-again site is a "news you can use" forum for Jihadists across the globe. The site's content is clearly incendiary. It promotes Holy War through the violent teachings of Abu Hamza al-Masri, the hook-handed, one-eyed former imam of London's Finsbury Park Mosque.

The Finsbury Park Mosque was where "Shoe Bomber" Richard Reid and other al Qaeda terrorists such as Zacarias Moussaoui once worshiped. This is more evidence that the secret Islamic terror network is hard at work reaching out as much through cyberspace as through prayer.

Television, radio, and newspapers are the most influential media outlets for terrorists—and these media are no strangers to supporting and influencing terrorist activities. The use of television to garner support for terrorists' causes, recruit supporters, and raise money began with Black September—an affiliate of the Popular Front for the Liberation of Palestine (PFLP)—which conducted a hostage-taking incident during the Olympic Games in Munich, West Germany, in September 1972. By carrying out the operation during the Olympic Games, Black September "starred" on every television network, constantly having its action on air and transmitting its message around the world. The media coverage created support for their cause and recruited volunteers. Black September understood, even then, one of today's media imperatives: "If it bleeds, it leads."

Now, in the twenty-first century, terrorists don't even have to time their actions to coincide with the physical presence of a media crew. Portable equipment, satellite telemetry, and worldwide 24/7 cable news competition have changed all that. Terrorism today always plays to a full house and standing room is guaranteed as hordes of cable news reporters descend to cover a story. News programming 24/7 necessitates hours of video interspersed with sound bites to attract viewers and to raise revenue. Cable networks live and die by ratings. All this, and Al-Jazeera, make for the "perfect storm" of terrorist coverage.

Al-Jazeera is financed by Sheik Hamad bin Khalifa al-Thani's family. Al-Thani is the emir of Qatar, where the network is based. More than 35 million Arabs, including 150,000 in this country, tune in every day to the Arabic-language network. Al-Jazeera hosts its own Web site, www.aljazeera.net, like many other television networks throughout the world. Based in Doha, with its sister TV station, www.aljazeera.net is the electronic version of the Al-Jazeera satellite channel. Although www.aljazeera.net is in Arabic, the greatest number of visitors to the site comes from the United States, owing to the lack of computers within the Arabic-speaking world. Al-Jazeera also has an English-language site, hosted in this country. The site was down for less than six hours after the raid by the North Texas Joint Terrorism Task Force on the offices of the INFOCOM Corporation.

Being "careful in its coverage of internal political issues of Arab Gulf countries," as Al-Jazeera describes itself on its Web site, doesn't apply to its coverage of America. It reported presidential candidate John Kerry's attacks on George W. Bush's White House without the clarification that it was campaign rhetoric, creating a distorted view of America and its politics for an Arab audience of 35 million. Imagine what someone unfamiliar with America would think after reading in the article "Al-Jazeera Praises Kerry": "[Kerry] says excluding France and Germany from rebuilding Iraq was 'dumb and insulting,'" and Al-Jazeera spotlighted Kerry's charge that the Bush Justice Department has stigmatized "innocent Muslims and Arabs who pose no danger."[9]

Al-Jazeera doesn't inform the millions of Arabs unfamiliar with America that Democracy is the sound of many voices and that we not only allow but encourage raucous debate in political contests. The Arab media's motive is to paint America as an evil oppressor. They do not report that there is neither free speech nor raucous debate where Islam rules. There aren't many political contests, either. The Koran is the law, and the leader is whoever's in charge of interpreting it.

There is evidence to support the possibility that the Al-Jazeera network might be acting as the voice of Osama bin Laden and al Qaeda. A little more than a month after 9/11, on October 21, 2001, Al-Jazeera conducted an interview with Osama bin Laden. A day before the interview took place, CNN reported that Vice President Dick Cheney strongly urged the network to behave responsibly when dealing with a suspected terrorist.[10]

Al-Jazeera didn't but CNN did.

This angered Al-Jazeera enough to break off ties with CNN, and within two weeks the Qatar-based network released two tapes, on November 3 and December 26. On the first, bin Laden predicted that the "U.S. government will lead the American people in and the West in general into an unbearable hell and a shocking life."[11]

Nick Berg's gruesome execution by Abu Musab al-Zarqawi should have dominated the news. But the first of several Americans to be beheaded by radical Islamic terrorists didn't. At the end of the day, Berg's execution was just another factoid. In the days following, more attention was paid to the ten suspended teachers across the country that showed the video in their classes than the events surrounding the execution.

The quick arrest of a few suspects in the beheading got hardly any coverage.

With the exception of the Fox News Channel, where Berg's execution was widely covered, reluctance to air the Berg tape failed to educate America about the cruel nature of our enemy. Conversely, the repeated broadcast of the pictures of prisoner abuse seemed to indicate a curious rush to convince America of the cruel nature of its own people. This, coupled with turning public opinion against the war in Iraq, plays so neatly into the enemy's hands that it is hard not to see that aim in the broadcasters' choices.

What we lose is a glimpse of the truth, unadulterated and clear. It is absolutely fair to judge America by its misconduct at the Abu Ghraib prison in Baghdad, for we are not a nation willing to torture an enemy to death; it is also absolutely fair to judge our Islamic enemies by a public beheading, for it clarifies how primitive and cruel it is within their nature to be.

On April 12, 2000, I was invited by the United Nations to address a distinguished panel of terrorism experts at the Ancillary Meeting at the Tenth United Nations Congress in Vienna, Austria. My speech, "The Impact of Terrorist Events in the Media on the Traumatization of Society," focused on how the media in the twenty-first century could traumatize, and thereby sway, society with their reporting of terrorist events.

The truth is that the ability of the media to utilize radio, television, and the Internet to reach every nook and cranny throughout the world with its terrorist images makes any trauma, everyone's trauma. Instantaneous, albeit repeated, media images can traumatize as effectively as a natural disaster.

Media imagery's relationship to trauma is understood by terrorists in America. Repeated images of jets flying into the World Trade Center carried on television and the Internet speaks to the increasing convergence of the place in which we live and function (the physical world) with the place in which data lives and functions (the virtual world). The new media technologies and competition for markets between news cable networks increase the repetitiveness of violent images made available to the general public. Each time we reach a new threshold, we somehow move willingly, albeit eagerly, to the next level. Desensitized, we escalate the cycle of violence to new heights.

Terrorism being communicated through our media, our media being used by terrorism in an ever-shrinking world, and the new protocols we will require to deal with the trauma witnessed by the new media technology will be increasingly as important as having to deal with the terrorist event itself.

For those who do not believe the secret network understands the influence of media, especially on the young, a story told about Omar Abdel-Rahman, the blind sheik convicted of influencing others to blow up a series of landmarks in New York, is on point: The sheik was asked by a youth about what to do about Western videos sold in a shop in Cairo. The sheik told the youth that heaven awaited those who with their own hands stopped the selling of blasphemous material. The youth was unsure of his ability to act alone, so he asked, "What if no one will help me and I can't do it?" The sheik answered the boy, "Just knowing the videos are evil does not assure one a place in heaven."

That night, the youth thought about his choices. The next morning he firebombed the video store.

CHAPTER 8

PROFILING

recently asked a high-ranking New York City cop if the flow of information from the feds to the local guys like him had gotten better since 9/11. He shook his head, "It still isn't happening." He said that despite things going on at local mosques, political correctness wasn't allowing the police departments to go near them. Also, there was more pressure than ever from the Department of Justice to avoid profiling. "How are we supposed to operate without profiling?" he asked, unsure how to protect the community if he couldn't identify its enemies.

It's not hard to see his point. Most of us still aren't sure why profiling terrorists isn't allowed. As researcher Michael Taarnby put it in his 2003 report for the Danish Ministry of Justice, "Profiling Islamic Suicide Terrorists"—"all Islamic suicide terrorists are Muslims, and this hardly constitutes any revelation."[1]

Wall Street Journal editor Jason L. Riley made it seem simple, too. "Of the nineteen hijackers responsible for [9/11's] calamity, all were Arabic, all were practitioners of Islam, and all came from known state incubators of terrorism in the Middle East. Of the twenty-two suspects on the FBI's 'most wanted' list of international terrorists, all are Arabic, all are practitioners of Islam, and all come from known state incubators of terrorism in the Middle East. Not 'some' of them, or a 'disproportionate number' of them. All of them."[2]

Americans believe profiling is a viable tool. After the September 11 attacks, 68 percent of Americans polled by the *Los Angeles Times* said they approved of "randomly stopping people who may fit the profile of suspected terrorists."[3] A CNN/*USA Today*/Gallup poll taken on October 1, 2001, found a majority of Americans agreed that people of Arab descent should "undergo special, more intensive security checks before boarding planes in the U.S."[4]

A *Boston Globe*/Gallup poll taken immediately after the 9/11 attacks found that even minority groups traditionally opposed to profiling now supported its use in the War on Terror—71 percent of African Americans polled favored profiling and stringent security checks for Arabs and Arab Americans at airports.[5]

Liberals immediately went on the attack, a knee-jerk reaction that ignored even their own constituencies. Their cynical assumption that 9/11 would be an "excuse" for the government to *abridge* civil rights rather than a *reason* to protect them was evident. The Leadership Conference on Civil Rights, the nation's largest and most diverse civil and human rights coalition of more than 180 national organizations—such as the Mexican

American Legal Defense and Educational Fund; the Citizens' Commission on Civil Rights; the Asian Pacific American Legal Consortium; the AFL-CIO; the American Association of People with Disabilities; and the Lawyers' Committee for Civil Rights Under Law—called for caution against racial, religious or ethnic scapegoating.

The ACLU report, "Sanctioned Bias: Racial Profiling Since 9/11," refers to a memo from "a group of senior U.S. intelligence specialists combating terrorism" mentioned in a Bill Dedham article in the *Boston Globe*.[6] The report quotes "one of the authors of the memo, all of whom spoke on condition of anonymity"[7]

> "If your goal is preventing attacks . . . you want your eyes and ears looking for pre-attack behaviors, not characteristics."[8]

Nice words, but what exactly are "pre-attack behaviors"? Do we tell law-enforcement agencies to wait until someone builds a bomb or hijacks an airplane again before we act? We already know that's too late—it was the way law-enforcement agencies operated *before* 9/11.

Without some kind of profiling, the police officers I spoke to told me they found it almost impossible to do their job. Lack of profiling made probable cause so vague that they couldn't act unless they saw a guy with a bomb in his hands. They were unable to anticipate an attack, plan countermeasures, or detect ongoing operations. Most of all, they were afraid of being attacked by liberals using any excuse to litigate their own agenda.

The most quarrelsome aspect of profiling has been on the local level, during routine traffic stops and encounters with state highway patrols and local police departments. This kind of racial profiling has been called "DWB"—"Driving While Black (or Brown)." It uses traffic violations as a pretext for stopping and searching black and Hispanic motorists to find evidence of more serious crimes, like possession of drugs or firearms.

A report by the Leadership Conference on Civil Rights "Wrong Then, Wrong Now: Racial Profiling Before and After September 11, 2001" argues:

> The assumptions driving terrorism profiling are the same as those behind traditional, street-level profiling—i.e., that a particular crime (here, terrorism) is most likely to be committed by members of a particular racial, ethnic or religious group, and that members of that group are, in general, likely to be involved in that kind of criminal activity.
>
> [It] is not true that terrorist acts are necessarily perpetrated by Arabs, or that the perpetrator of a terrorist act is likely to be an Arab. While all the men involved in the September 11 hijackings were Arab nationals, Richard Reid, who on December 22, 2001, tried to ignite an explosive device on a trans-Atlantic flight, was a British citizen of Jamaican ancestry. Prior to September 11, the bloodiest act of terrorism on United States soil was perpetrated by Timothy McVeigh. Non-Arabs like John Walker Lindh can be found in the ranks of the Taliban, al Qaeda, and other terrorist organizations.[9]

This is one more case of ignoring the facts to undermine the logic of terrorist profiling. Of the twenty-two examples "supporting" the proposition, "It is not true that terrorist acts are necessarily perpetrated by Arabs, or that the perpetrator of a terrorist act is likely to be an Arab," twenty-one of the twenty-two above-mentioned terrorists were Muslim; nineteen of twenty-two were Arab; all of the nineteen 9/11 hijackers were Arab *and* Muslim; both Richard Reid and John Walker Lindh were converts to Islam; and Lindh, who studied Islam in Yemen then joined the Taliban, according to the criminal complaint filed in the United States District Court for the Eastern District of Virginia, began his jihad on the front lines north of Kabul, and later was sent to fight in the province of Takhar right before the war began.

The ACLU main-page summary on "Immigrants Rights" states that "every wave of immigration has faced fear and hostility, especially during times of economic hardship, political turmoil, or war."[10]

• In 1882, Congress passed the Chinese Exclusion Act to keep out all people of Chinese origin.

• In the 1920s, the "Red Scare" accused thousands of foreign-born people of political radicalism, and many were arrested, brutalized, and deported without a hearing.

• In 1942, 120,000 Americans of Japanese descent were interned in camps until the end of World War II.

Internment camps were heinous—they happened sixty years ago, once. The Red Scare was heinous—it was eighty years ago.

The Chinese Exclusion Act was repealed in 1943. Since then, we've grown up a lot. The results are that George W. Bush's administration has more minorities and women in senior positions than any administration before it and legal remedies afforded protected classes are greater and more extensive than ever before.

The Bush administration's racial-profiling guidelines bar federal law-enforcement officials from engaging in racial profiling—even where profiling would be permitted by the Constitution. The guidelines apply to all federal law-enforcement activities. However, included therein is a rational "exemption" to the guidelines in cases of national security.

"The policy makes a clear distinction between routine law enforcement work and that involving national security or border security," wrote Curt Anderson of the Associated Press. "Authorities can subject certain ethnic or racial groups to greater scrutiny if there is specific information that such people are preparing to mount a terrorist attack (or) when there is trustworthy information, relevant to the locality or time-frame at issue that links persons of a particular race or ethnicity to an identified criminal incident, scheme or organization."[11] That means adult males from the Middle East can draw greater attention at airports if the government uncovers a plot by al Qaeda to bomb U.S. airliners.

To the ACLU and other liberal organizations the exemption is just another government conspiracy. The ACLU stated:

• "The very inclusion of a national security exception in the guidelines is an admission by the Department of Justice that it relies upon racial and ethnic profiling in its domestic counter-terrorism efforts."[12]

• "It looks to me like that it is more interested in carving out exceptions to racial profiling than it is in enforcing a ban," said Miriam Gohara, an attorney with the NAACP Legal Defense Fund.[13]

• "The guidance includes broad wording like 'national security,' which makes the motivation and purpose of the policy unclear," according to Wade Henderson, executive director of The Leadership Conference on Civil Rights.[14]

• "It gives carte blanche to federal law-enforcement officers to continue racially and ethnically profiling people in situations deemed to be of 'national security concern' by federal law enforcement, including, and most troubling, in all immigration-related situations, such as in airports and on the border," said National Council of La Raza president Raul Yzaguirre.[15]

• Karen K. Narasaki, president and executive director of the National Asian Pacific American Legal Consortium, complained, "Without a means of enforcement by allowing targets to be chosen by religion and national origin, and by carving out an exception that easily swallows the rule, the attorney general ignores the president's promise to end racial profiling."[16]

National Security Advisor Condoleezza Rice testified to the 9/11 Commission, "We're at war, it's a war we have to win, and it is a war that cannot be fought on the defensive. It's a war that has to be fought on the offense." Former U.S. attorney general

Janet Reno told the 9/11 Commission on April 13, "Everything that has been done in the Patriot Act has been helpful, I think, while at the same time maintaining the balance with respect to civil liberties."

It was never in doubt that liberal groups would oppose the USA Patriot Act, but it is imperative that we don't let it expire. It's our only hope the FBI and the CIA will combine intelligence. It permits the surveillance of mosques for the first time and allows law enforcement to keep up with the bad guys, technologically speaking.

Roving wiretaps are necessary in an age of cellular phone technology. They were illegal until the Patriot Act. The old laws worked when the cord on the black metal family phone wouldn't let you move more than a couple of feet. Roving wiretaps are necessary to intercept and track terrorists using satellite phones.

The Patriot Act gives the Department of Justice the same tools to investigate terrorism as law-enforcement agencies use to investigate crime. After a federal grand jury in Buffalo indicted the Lackawanna 6 on charges including conspiracy to provide material support to terrorists, Attorney General John Ashcroft called the Patriot Act "the key weapon used across America in successful counter-terrorist operations."[17] He told a House committee, "The Department used confidential informants to gather facts; we used subpoenas to collect travel information to track their movements; we deployed surveillance to record conversations; we used search warrants to locate weapons and jihad materials; and we used some of the best interrogators from the FBI to obtain critical admissions from some of the defendants."[18]

Ashcroft further stated that criminal plea agreements, many under seal, from more than fifteen individuals have provided critical intelligence about al Qaeda and other terrorist groups about weapons stored in the United States, locations scouted for attacks by al Qaeda, safe houses, training camps, recruitment, terrorist tactics in the United States and operations against American citizens.[19]

The Patriot Act deserves credit for the arrest of members of previously mentioned terrorist cells in Buffalo, Seattle, Portland, and Detroit, and investigations of terrorists have frozen $125 million in terrorist assets and over six hundred bank accounts around the world. I believe the Patriot Act has the right balances in the sometimes-competing interests of the War on Terror and our civil liberties. If we are to prevent a terrorist attack of major proportions, it is essential. Usually, in law enforcement we wait until a crime is committed, and then we act. America cannot afford to wait until a terrorist act is committed to go after the terrorists who commit them.

One of the problems with profiling is that liberals have made it almost impossible to use and as a consequence we aren't very good at it. One suburban New York police academy created a terrorist profile derived from the "Al Qaeda Training Manual" mentioned in chapter 3. From the manual:

Security precautions related to apartments:

Choosing the apartment carefully as far as the location, the size for the work necessary (meetings, storage, arms, fugitives, work preparation).

It is preferable to rent apartments on the ground floor to facilitate escape and digging of trenches.

Preparing secret locations in the apartment for securing documents, records, arms, and other important items.

It is preferable to rent these apartments using false names, appropriate cover, and non-Moslem appearance.

If there is a telephone in the apartment, calls should be answered in an agreed-upon manner among those who use the apartment. That would prevent mistakes that would, otherwise, lead to revealing the names and nature of the occupants.

For apartments, replacing the locks and keys with new ones.

When selecting an arsenal, consider the following:

The arsenal should not be in well-protected areas, or close to parks or public places.

The arsenal should not be a room that is constantly used and cannot be given up by family members who do not know the nature of the father or husband's work.

Measures that should be taken by the overt member:

He should not carry on him the names and addresses of those members he knows. If he has to, he should keep them safe.

During times of security concerns and arrest campaigns and
especially if his appearance is Islamic, he should reduce his
visits to the areas of trouble and remain at home instead.
When conversing on the telephone, he should not talk about
any information that might be of use to the enemy.

The manual is a fascinating document—and frightening,
considering the level of preparation it indicates. The following
is what's taught to rookies at the police academy, in the "Patrol
Tactics and Prevention" section of their training manual titled
Terrorism: Awareness, Prevention, Response (see the appendix).

**The following is a partial list of behavioral indicators that
were taken from instructions in the al Qaeda Manual:**

Assume "Americanized" appearance

Remain armed while transporting organizational funds

Carry false or forged identification

Obtain passports from countries other than the United States

Seek apartment rentals on the first floor, towards the middle of the
complex (for escape purposes)

Seek apartment rentals in transient or new neighborhoods

Replace locks and keys upon renting apartments

Utilize public phones in busy areas

Travel during the day

Draw detailed diagrams of potential targets

Take panoramic pictures of potential targets

Unfortunately, if police officers actually look for a terrorist
based on these indicators, as the manual suggests, the suspect

would be an armed American-looking type carrying a fake ID who lives in a first-floor apartment in the middle of a new complex or an old tenement, has no phones but new locks, and likes to draw and take pictures.

The 9/11 hijackers don't fit that profile. Terrorists like Khalid "Shaikh" Mohammed don't fit that profile. Neither does Osama bin Laden. In fact, except for being armed, the people it most fits are college kids below the drinking age.

This kind of training gives the street cop very little useful information, and most complain there is simply no way to know what job to do, or how to do it. The intuition his or her experience has bred is unnerved by conflicting social, political, and legal forces. He figures a Muslim terrorist might look Middle Eastern or Arabic, but he's told that thinking like that is profiling, and it's wrong. He might want to verify someone's ID with certain tests that use nothing but light to reveal symbols or watermarks, or signs of an altered original—which most forged IDs are—but can't because he or she doesn't want to be accused of singling out someone unless the suspect is damn close to being an armed American-looking type carrying fake ID who lives in a first-floor apartment with new locks and no phones in the middle of a new complex or an old tenement, who likes to draw and take pictures.

On the other hand, abridging the rights of an entire group always relies on how easy it is for those doing the abridging to let others suffer what they would hate to suffer themselves, and it includes the historically foolish trust that they never will. H. L. Mencken said, "For every problem, there is a solution that is simple, neat, and wrong."

When the Rhode Island Superior Court turned down Aaron Lopez's and Isaac Elizer's naturalization applications for citizenship, the men refused to accept the decision and appealed to the lower house of the Rhode Island legislature for redress. Grudgingly, the legislature approved the naturalization applications, but:

> Inasmuch as the said Aaron Lopez hath declared himself by religion a Jew, this Assembly doth not admit himself nor any other of that religion to the full freedom of this Colony. So that the said Aaron Lopez nor any other of said religion is not liable to be chosen into any office in this colony nor allowed to give vote as a free man in choosing others.

The case was reheard in Superior Court on March 11, 1762. The court reasoned that Parliament had authorized naturalization in the colonies to increase population, but Rhode Island had become so crowded that it no longer applied there.

> Further by the charter granted to this colony, it appears that the free and quiet enjoyment of the Christian religion and a desire of propagating the same were the principal views with which this colony was settled, and by a law made and passed in the year 1663, no person who does not profess the Christian religion can be admitted free [that is, as a voter or office holder] to this colony.

Liberals who attack the Patriot Act couldn't do a better job of aiding and abetting the enemy if they tried. Militant Islam loves the conflict, using charges of government abuse and racism to confirm that Muslims in America are a persecuted group and should be afraid.

Does it surprise anyone that the Islamic-controlled media does not report the Patriot Act favorably? A December 15, 2003, Al-Jazeera article by Benjamin Duncan in Washington, D.C., "Fears over USA Patriot Act" quotes the following:

• "For many, the Patriot Act is now a symbol of draconian government laws in the post 9/11 era," said Nancy Talanian, director of the Bill of Rights Defence Committee, an advocacy group based in Massachusetts.

• "Our fears are that we still do not even know how it is being used and that is even more frightening to me," said Laila al-Qatami, spokeswoman for the American-Arab Anti-Discrimination Committee, a civil rights group in Washington.

• Those opposed to the Patriot Act are faced with the challenge of substantiating their criticism of the law's potential for abuse with hard evidence of its enforcement, a problem noted by former Republican congressman Bob Barr in testimony before the Senate Judiciary Committee in mid-November.

• In an effort to break down the veil of secrecy surrounding the law, the American Civil Liberties Union (ACLU) filed a Freedom of Information Act (FOIA) request in August of 2002.[20]

The article goes on: "Perhaps the most scrutinized section of the Patriot Act is Section 215, which made it easier for the government to secretly obtain personal documents such as financial, library, medical, phone and Mosque records with less stringent judicial oversight."[21]

Section 215 has been the target of civil rights groups who worry federal authorities could and would use it to target anyone who the government felt was threatening. However, Section 215 has never been used. In September, U.S. Attorney General John Ashcroft said Section 215 had not been used. Company spokeswoman Patty Smith said that Amazon.com, the Internet retailing giant, has never received a request under Section 215.[22]

The Al-Jazeera article continues:

• Al-Jazeera reports many civil rights advocates having said, "Just because the Justice Department said it has not used Section 215 does not mean it is not having a negative impact on certain communities."

• "It doesn't even have to be used, let alone abused," ACLU President Nadine Strossen told the Senate Judiciary Committee in November.

• Strossen is quoted as having said that the mere existence of Section 215 was creating a chilling effect among many Muslim Americans who "stopped expressing their political views because they are afraid that this power can be used against them."

• "It has become, to some people, in some ways, a whipping boy for a whole host of other abuses," said Nancy Talanian. "For critics of the Bush administration who view the detentions at Guantanamo Bay as unlawful, and the hundreds of deportation cases involving Arabs and Muslims as grossly unjust, the Patriot Act is a battle cry for civil rights violations in America."[23]

I like "a symbol of draconian government laws in the post-9/11 era" a lot. "Those opposed to the Patriot Act are faced with the challenge of substantiating their criticism of the law's potential for abuse with hard evidence of its enforcement, a problem . . ."—that's okay, too. But my personal favorites are "Just because the Justice Department said it has not used Section 215 does not mean it is not having a negative impact on certain communities" and ACLU President Nadine Strossen's statement, "It doesn't even have to be used, let alone abused."

It's hard to get this much nonsense into such a small piece. What isn't nonsense are the lessons about terrorism I've learned over the years. I advocate profiling because I consider the danger to America posed by terrorists, and the possibility of their using weapons of mass destruction or germ warfare against us, to outweigh all other concerns. Profiling at our airports and borders and in seaports can lessen that threat, and if that's what it takes to protect us, I will be first in line to be profiled, too.

CHAPTER 9

GOVERNMENT AGENCIES

was appointed Terrorism Analyst for the U.S. Federal Probation Department in January 2002. My job description read in part: "You agree to offer your expertise to our staff, especially our newly created Surveillance Unit." The Chief Probation Officer had seen the increasing presence of terrorists in the community and created the unit in response.

The Chief's first worried letter contained this sentence: "We are obligated to supervise suspected terrorists who are on parole or probation." A follow-up letter added a significant word: "Our officers supervise both *known* or suspected terrorists who are on parole or probation." The word "known" told me how fast the threat level was rising. That's why I was appointed.

I had been training department personnel as far back as the mid-1990s when the first concerns about terrorism emerged. Now the Chief wanted me to train the Surveillance Unit officers to recognize possible terrorist activity when they were in the field, or visiting clients' homes, often in densely populated Arab communities. What might be indicators of terrorist activity? What should the officer look for? What questions might the officer ask? What could be used as evidence?

The unit consisted of an Organized Crime Specialist and officers who had supervised drug cases. It would watch offenders who were suspected of being terrorists, a small but important part of the Probation Department's two main divisions: Pre-Sentence investigated individuals after conviction, but before sentencing, and wrote the pre-sentence report, applying our complex federal guidelines to the offense so the judge could reach a sentence; Supervision monitored felons who were on probation.

In one case we discussed, the officers felt they were overlooking something in the home of a convicted extremist under their supervision. They suspected he had become active again but needed evidence to prove it. The offender's profile and habits suggested to me he was in contact with terrorist groups. I urged the officers to check his e-mails and other files on his computer. The search yielded evidence of a conspiracy to commit another terrorist act. His probation was violated and he went back to jail.

There was one other hand-picked group in the department. The Special Offenders Unit was created in 1978 to watch career criminals. These were felons who had historically pursued criminal activities as a primary means of their livelihood, including those individuals who have extensive arrest records, affiliations with organized crime and gangs, high-level narcotics offenders, terrorist organizations, or other offenders suspected of involvement in criminal activity.

The unit had six officers to supervise 250 offenders. The officers were seasoned veterans from a variety of ethnic groups. They also supervised Witness Security Cases (WITSEC). Their training included the use of surveillance, financial investigations, and informants. As a by-product of these activities, they also gathered intelligence.

Most Americans don't know that immediately after 9/11, the FBI asked all crime-related federal agencies for a list of "individuals of concern" from "countries of interest" who were under their jurisdiction. The list was to include predominantly Arab or Muslim felons involved in activities associated with terrorism—money laundering, drug trafficking, and documents counterfeiting. One of the first agencies the FBI sought out to get information was the Special Offenders Unit of the Federal Probation Department.

The SOU was happy to comply (see the appendix). However, the moment the unit delivered files, the FBI stopped working with them. The wall that went up never came down. To this day, no one in the department or the SOU has ever been told the result of the investigations. This weakens a law-enforcement agency by implying their officers aren't capable of handling sensitive investigations. No individual or agency wants to be treated like a poor relation.

A common feeling among federal officers is that working with the FBI means giving all your information and getting nothing back. The FBI pursues a case only if it controls it completely. One federal officer put it like this: "The FBI doesn't share anything with anybody. They take but they don't give."

What makes this somewhat ironic is that all federal probation officers have to be vetted by the FBI, and the security examination is far more comprehensive than for local or state police officers.

Despite the unit's potential value to the War on Terrorism, they aren't used as an asset. SOU and the Surveillance Unit could aid local police authorities in cases where the status of an individual under arrest is unclear or there are suspicions of terrorist activity. Federal Probation could be part of a more effective identification system than using driver's license or Social Security numbers, which are much too easy to buy or steal. Yet Probation doesn't have the budget or the means to do the job and continues to report failed contacts with the INS and the FBI; the population of illegal alien felons with links to terrorism continues to grow; and the time and money spent on them bankrupts our criminal justice system.

On March 1, 2003, the former Immigration and Naturalization Service (INS) was incorporated into the new Department of Homeland Security. The new DHS is a complicated endeavor and deserves a chance to prove itself. However, combining agencies to end duplication of services, transfer intelligence more efficiently, retool civil servants, and create new missions simply won't work. By its own admission during the 9/11 hearings, DHS won't be effective for years. The danger is that it may *never* be effective. The new agency will contain the same self-styled experts who failed to connect the dots for the last twenty years. What makes us think a bureaucratic reshuffling will have different results?

> It is not only common sense that makes clear the inherent relationship between enforcing the immigration laws and considerations of both foreign policy and national security; rather, those considerations are embedded in the text of the immigration laws themselves.
>
> INA § 237(a)(4)(C)(i), 8 U.S.C.Legal Opinion issued on February 20, 2003, *The Limitations On The Detention Authority Of The INS*

A noble sentiment, but it isn't even close to reality. A letter sent to me from a high-level official at the New York Asylum Office gave me the real skinny—"Many of our applicants testify to having committed terrorist acts. Sometimes we have reason to believe they committed such acts even when they do not so testify" (see the appendix).

In addition, the official told me many of the applicants the office sees present bogus credentials. Some of the applicants have spent time in the Afghan terrorist training camps funded by Osama bin Laden—they are all walking time bombs and should be denied entry. That requires asking the FBI to check if the applicant's name is on the terrorist Watch List.

Only the FBI has the Watch List. Without it, Asylum officials have almost no choice but to grant temporary entry visas to these applicants and release them on their own recognizance. As might be expected, most are never seen again.

Another very highly placed federal official based in Florida I had worked with and knew quite well told me in the spring of 2004, "It's a thousand times worse now than before 9/11. Now that INS has merged with Border Patrol, the new configuration doesn't have anything to do with each other. INS doesn't want to do the job of the Border Patrol people, and vice versa. Nobody seems to be in charge. For example, you talk to one person one day, and call back the next, that person is no longer available. One day you might get an INS person, the second a Border Patrol guy, the third, a different INS person. There's no transition, no continuity."[1]

His biggest beef was with the FBI. Not surprisingly, it was about getting information. "Look, money is tight," he told me. "You spend it on surveillance, then turn the results over to the FBI and never hear anything about it again. Resources are scarce. You want to know if these are the right variables to use in the future. There's no way to know if what you found out was important, no way to measure performance."[2]

Is the FBI the real problem? Maybe it's just protecting information that would compromise agents and their investigations. The Bureau is so insular that its inner workings are known to only a few. Agency lore has long held that the famed FBI psychological profiling unit was created just so FBI agents wouldn't have to go to outside the Bureau to see a psychologist.

Like the old Tom Lehrer song about the French hating the Germans and the Germans hating the Dutch, and so on—the Probation Department hates the INS, the INS hates federal court officers, and everybody seems to have a problem with the FBI, even local law-enforcement personnel. An encounter with a New York City police sergeant on duty at ground zero a few days after 9/11 stands out in my mind. He called me over and asked if I knew anything about what was going on. I told him he probably knew more than I did. He shook his head. "The FBI tells us nothing. They're even more tight-lipped than before this shit happened."

My own experience with the FBI wasn't much different. About ten years ago I approached the FBI and the U.S. Department of Justice with a proposal for a toll-free national tip line for terrorism. I was representing Crime Stoppers International, the umbrella organization for the thousand-plus crime-stoppers units worldwide that solved hundreds of thousands of felony crimes. One prominent agent told me that the FBI wasn't interested in what he called "anonymous tips." "What happens if we get an anonymous tip about some Arab blowing up a building and we don't check it out? We'll get sued. Thanks, but no thanks. We'll stick with the known assets we can trust."

I had another, more personal encounter with the Bureau. They asked me to work for them locating terrorists who might have infiltrated the university system. I am a counterterrorism expert who has trained the FBI and have letters of gratitude to prove it. However, the agents made it clear that my relationship to the Bureau would be no different than any other "asset."

Their trust in me would be based on the quality of information I gave them, but I would always be an outsider and would serve without the right to question, analyze, or contribute to the larger picture.

That's why so many law-enforcement officers are reluctant to work with the FBI. Like me, these officers are committed to protecting the community, but, like me, they want to be treated in a professional manner, something the FBI seems unable to do even after all these years.

The fault doesn't lie totally with the FBI. The FBI had long used its own criteria for intelligence collection and was given almost unlimited authority by U.S. attorneys general. Yet stung by criticism during the Watergate hearings, and the involvement of their Acting Director L. Patrick Gray, a Nixon-appointee, the FBI found itself subjected to congressional investigation.

Following congressional hearings, Attorney General Edward Levi gave the FBI detailed guidelines for the first time. Priorities were shifted. The number of case files was sharply reduced. The FBI could only open a case file on a person who had committed a crime, or about whom there was compelling evidence that he or she was about to commit one.

Almost overnight, the FBI had to change from an "intelligence gathering" agency to a "crime-solving" agency. In the wake of 9/11, we've asked them to change back again. The trouble is, before 9/11 the FBI suffered embarrassments in highly publicized cases, such as Ruby Ridge, Waco, and the Unabomber investigations. It's made them gun-shy.

The Bureau also dropped the ball on the 1993 bombing of the World Trade Center when it failed to investigate documents seized after the assassination of Rabbi Meir Kahane in 1990. El Sayyid Nosair killed Kahane in a meeting room of the Marriott Halloran House Hotel in midtown Manhattan on November 5, 1990. Nosair's apartment yielded a treasure trove of documents, in Arabic, but they weren't even translated till years later. When they were translated, they included plans for attacking the World Trade Center.

Ruby Ridge involved the surveillance of the Randy Weaver family atop Ruby Ridge, Idaho. Weaver, a white separatist, was wanted by the federal marshals for failing to appear in court on a weapons charge. After the FBI stakeout went sour, Weaver's wife and son were killed. The government had to pay Weaver for his loss.

A year later, more than eighty people perished at the Branch Davidian Compound at Mount Carmel just outside Waco, Texas. A fire ignited by the FBI's teargas shells or the Davidians themselves, burned the compound to the ground. The FBI again was embarrassed for their actions in this operation. As for the Unabomber case, it lasted two decades and might still have been unsolved had the Unabomber's brother not turned him in.

In some ways 9/11 made the FBI only more self-conscious and protective of their image. They were always reticent about giving information. After 9/11 whatever came into their possession never left it. I have spoken to many state and local agencies or departments charged with protecting American citizens where they live and work. Almost all report their biggest problem in the War on Terrorism is nobody giving them up-to-date information about threats from the Islamic terror network. Most say even three years after 9/11, the FBI and related federal intelligence and law-enforcement agencies still don't "download" real-time information to local agencies.

On April 8, 2004, National Security Advisor Dr. Condoleezza Rice had the following exchange with Commissioner Fred F. Fielding, former counsel to the president of the United States, during her testimony before the National Commission on Terrorist Attacks Upon the United States:

Fielding: It doesn't appear to us, even with the changes up until now, that it's solved the institutional versus institutional issues.

Rice: Every day now in the Oval Office in the morning, the FBI director and the CIA director sit with the president, sharing information in ways that they would have been prohibited to share that information before.

Fielding: It may be solved at the top. We've got to make sure it's solved at the bottom.

Rice: I agree completely.

The trouble is neither Homeland Security nor any other federal agency is doing anything to create resources at the "bottom" other than ignoring valuable assets we could use in the War on Terrorism. Intelligence is not collected at the "top." In the case of the secret Islamic network, it must be collected on the streets of our cities. That's where terrorists live and operate. That's where operations are planned and executed.

Homeland Security and the FBI have to develop assets who can collect and deliver real-time information on the ground—the communities housing al Qaeda terrorists. A viable intelligence operation requires information from reliable sources. Specific targets and directed operations can then be considered, ordered, and executed.

"In hindsight," Rice said, "if anything might have helped stop 9/11, it would have been better information about threats inside the United States." All that means is we may wait till doomsday for the FBI and CIA to cooperate, and in the meantime it won't be creating the assets they need on the ground.

Yet federal law-enforcement agencies haven't gone back to important sources of information like the Probation Department's Special Offender Unit and Surveillance Unit since the days right after 9/11. There are other important but unused sources. United States Postal Service mail carriers don't usually announce how well our mail identifies our personal web of people and organizations. Mail carriers can spot mail drops. They can tell how many people live at an address. They can tell your interests and your family's. Investigators call it "mail cover," and in one case helped send a felon suspected of terrorism who was out on probation back into jail.

Federal laws still constrain probation officers on routine visits to the homes of Middle Eastern illegal-alien felons they supervise from asking questions of, or investigating, any of the other people who live there, not even if they are illegal aliens also, not even if two fall out of a hidden closet—which happened to an officer I've known personally for many years.

In 1999, I conducted an in-depth study for the U.S. Probation Department, Eastern District of New York. The Eastern District includes the New York City boroughs of Brooklyn, Queens, and Staten Island, and the Long Island counties of Nassau and Suffolk. The total population exceeds 8 million people, and this is the jurisdiction where both LaGuardia and JFK International airports are located, a prime point of entry into America.

I created a set of statistics describing the criminal offenders who were under the Probation Department's supervision using the records of 6,333 cases active from March 1, 1997, through February 28, 1998. I found over 27 percent of the entire offender population were legal or illegal aliens, with an additional 22 percent of the population citizenship status classified as "unknown." That means almost 50 percent of the offender population aren't American citizens. Along with draining the department's resources and taxpayers' money, the study found that illegal aliens were less likely than all others to satisfy their special conditions of supervision.

Accused felons are supposed to be tried in a federal court because immigration violations are federal crimes. If guilty, they are supposed to serve time in jail, and then be deported. However, if the illegal alien has almost *any* kind of ID—nothing fancy, a driver's license or a Social Security card—he'll be placed in the state or local jail facility, and tried in a state or local court. After jail time, he will be released back into the community. If he doesn't receive jail time, he'll be gone that much sooner.

I interviewed a New York City Legal Aid lawyer with two decades of experience in immigration cases. Her clients are not wealthy. She rarely meets them in her office. Most often she first sees them in jail, where the police have taken them right from the airport or the incident. She told me how INS's search for illegal aliens in the prison population really works.

"Assume for a moment you're arrested at Kennedy Airport for a violation that is not a federal crime, or that the U.S. attorney has no interest in prosecuting," she said. "You're kicked to the New York State criminal justice system, or the New York City criminal justice system. Believe it or not, felons in the state prison system get randomly called down from their cells to an interview room where an INS official asks them if they are illegal aliens. They need not answer. Most don't. In fact, they don't even have to go to the interview if they don't want to—and most are smart enough to know it.[3]

"Defense attorneys have an obligation to warn clients against self-incrimination, so they must advise their clients not to answer the INS's questions 'voluntarily.'" She knew some defense attorneys who told illegals to lie to the INS, but there were enough jailhouse lawyers to guarantee that anyway. With this kind of slipshod system, she said, "INS misses at least fifty percent of illegal aliens who are in state prisons. It misses *one hundred percent* of illegal aliens released on bail. Why? Well, they just disappear."[4]

With INS so easy to fool or avoid, many illegals are released into the community after they serve their sentence, or are given probation and told to get a job. Federal judges have actually made finding a job a condition of probation for illegal aliens and have issued work permits. Illegal-alien felons with terrorist connections should not be given parole or probation, or allowed to go to work. They should be deported in the ninety-day time frame federal law establishes or serve their full sentence, and then be deported.

The August 1999 Civic Report, "'Broken Windows' Probation: The Next Step in Fighting Crime," from the Reinventing Probation Council, makes that point, too. "If the criminal justice system is going to keep violent crime on the run . . . it will need to do even more, beginning with a much better job of supervising the three million probationers in our midst."[5]

In the middle of 2003, a record-breaking total of approximately 6.8 million offenders were under some form of correctional supervision—in prison, in jail, on probation, or on parole. Of these, more than 4.8 million were adults on probation or parole, or just under 71 percent of the entire offender population. This means on any given day there are almost 5 million probationers or parolees living in communities across the land. More than half have been convicted of felony violations of the law.

What has to be done, the report suggests, is to enforce violations of probation conditions quickly and strongly because probationers often realize that they may expect two or more "free ones" when it comes to dirty urine samples, electronic-monitoring violations, or failure to comply with a variety of supervision conditions. This means all conditions of a probation sentence must be enforced, and all violations must be responded to in a timely fashion.

Further, the response must be swift and sure. This does not mean that each violation will result in the revocation of probation, but rather the imposition of graduated sanctions (for example, curfew or house arrest, electronic monitoring, mandatory drug treatment). Probation agencies need to be tough-minded and put teeth into apprehending absconders from probation. If it is easier for an offender to abscond than to comply with the terms and conditions of probation, they will.

The federal court system cannot be allowed to abdicate all responsibility for what happens outside the courtroom. Judges cannot continue to put illegal aliens with felony records and terrorist ties back into the community just because they have no idea what else to do.

One federal judge sentenced an illegal alien convicted of smuggling heroin, later referred to the FBI for suspicions of terrorist links, to thirty months in jail, three years on probation, a one-hundred-dollar special assessment, and two hundred hours of community service. What sort of community service does a convicted heroin smuggler suspected of being a terrorist get? He was assigned to help out in the Queens Botanical Gardens (see the appendix).

He hasn't been there in three years.

My somewhat whimsical solution to the problem of countries that refuse to take back their citizens who entered America illegally: I suggest we lower the number of legal immigrants we allow from their country into our country on a two-for-one basis. If we normally take ten people in, and the other country refuses to take back two people we want to deport, we lower their legal immigration limit from ten to six.

But the liberal media explodes with rage when anyone questions the changing face of America. People whisper when they say things like, "I remember when cabbies spoke English" or "Gas stations used to be run by people capable of giving directions." "America used to be able to pull together. Why not now?" Are these the words of bigots who forget how their own immigrant ancestors had to make their way up the economic ladder, or wistful memories of better days?

America has changed. In the past, immigrants to these shores were escaping famine, poverty, or death. The streets weren't paved with gold, their dreams were. "If you built a bridge to the old country, I wouldn't drive back," said one old man to me. America was home. They saved pennies to bring the rest of the family "over," not to go back.

Technology changed things. It became cheap and simple to communicate with people still in the homeland—which is what makes it dangerous to America. Anyone can use a phone card or the Internet to do business or get information. Low-cost transportation changes things, too. Cheap airline tickets make it possible to do "business" in Peshawar—a city in Pakistan where AK-47 assault rifles outnumber cell phones—and sleep in New York the following day.

The impact of so many Muslims arriving so quickly exaggerates their presence. American society is impatient with immigrants failing to join the collective. It's not always a seamless transition for Muslims. Unlike Christianity, Islam and Judaism contain a legal code delineating daily conduct. Christianity is about salvation—the redemptive power of deliverance from the penalty of original sin. Judaism and Islam are about rules.

Jews came to America to save their lives. A minority overseas, they remained a minority. Jewish law had to be flexible enough to accommodate that reality. Islam demands obedience. America's lack of a mandated belief system, and its separation of Church and State, can be "proof" to Muslims that secular rule will destroy their culture. For many, the only alternative is a return to fundamental Islam.

Noted scholar Bernard Lewis put it this way in his book *What Went Wrong?*:

> If the peoples of Middle East continue on their present path, the suicide bomber may become a metaphor for the whole region, and there will be no escape from a downward spiral of hate and spite, rage and self-pity, [and] poverty and oppression.

No one is stepping up to the plate to deal with another highly charged issue—immigration. On the contrary, the ACLU and other liberals are busy defending the rights of illegals, oblivious of their crimes or their victims. America should require a commitment to the Constitution and the secular nature of our country, as well as an understanding of its cultural expectations. Our system of preference for immigrants should welcome those who accept our definition of good citizenship and reject those with records of criminal activity, anti-Americanism, or any link to terrorism.

Every year, the entry visas of thousands of foreign students expire, but the students remain in the United States. No one is quite sure when an "order of removal" (deportation) will be issued, but when it is, the INS sends a notice to the student asking them to please come back and turn themselves in to be deported. It is often referred to as a "run letter" because, as you might imagine, 87 percent of deportable aliens who get these letters run. The figure on foreign students disappearing after their visas expire rises to 94 percent if they are from countries linked to terrorism.

The result? A very highly placed official from a federal agency in Florida recently told me that President Bush is so worried about alienating the Hispanic community that supports him, he won't let them deport Hispanic illegal aliens. This sends a mixed message, and a conflict with "equal protection," so these agencies can't try to deport militant Islamic terrorists, either. The result is they are unable to act at all.

America is an immigrant nation, but at this critical moment in our development we need to ensure the dominance of Western values. Unconditional immigration strains resources beyond endurance. The Bureau of Labor may tell us we need more immigration, but an "inner voice" reminds us we need to sustain certain values along with it, like the English language, compliance with the law, and respect for American institutions and traditions.

Journalist Heather MacDonald wrote in the Winter 2004 issue of *City Journal:*

Even when immigration officials actually arrest someone, and even if a judge issues a final deportation order (usually after years of litigation and appeals), they rarely have the manpower to put the alien on a bus or plane and take him across the border. Second alternative: detain him pending removal. Again, inadequate space and staff. In the early 1990s, for example, 15 INS officers were in charge of the deportation of approximately 85,000 aliens in New York City.

To other law-enforcement agencies, the feds' triage often looks like complete indifference to immigration violations. Testifying to Congress about the Queens rape by illegal Mexicans, New York's criminal justice coordinator defended the city's failure to notify the INS after the rapists' previous arrests on the ground that the agency wouldn't have responded anyway. "We have time and time again been unable to reach INS on the phone," John Feinblatt said last February. "When we reach them on the phone, they require that we write a letter. When we write a letter, they require that it be by a superior."

Criminal aliens also interpret the triage as indifference. John Mullaly, a former NYPD homicide detective, estimates 70 percent of the drug dealers and other criminals in Manhattan's Washington Heights were illegal. Were Mullaly to threaten an illegal-alien thug in custody that his next stop would be El Salvador unless he cooperated, the criminal would just laugh, knowing that the INS would never show up. The message could not be clearer: this is a culture that can't enforce its most basic law of entry. If the "broken windows" theory is correct—that visible signs of a community in disorder, such as broken windows or abandoned vehicles, breeds a downward spiral of decay and lawlessness—then America's visible failure to enforce *most* of its laws will continue to breed contempt for *all* of its laws.

If you live in an American city, there are terrorists living nearby. Those who still think that isn't true should be aware of the population supervised by a probation officer I knew quite well. Within his "clients" was an alleged "sleeper" who told interviewers that he knew nine of the nineteen 9/11 hijackers. The subject was an illegal alien whose student visa had expired years before. He had been convicted of Social Security fraud. He had been reported to the FBI. He had been ordered deported by the court.

At present, he lives on Staten Island.

FINAL THOUGHTS AND SUGGESTIONS

Over fifty thousand Muslims went through the Afghan terrorist-training camps Osama bin Laden built. He taught them all, "It is a sin not to use any capability in defense of Islam." So far, that has included bombs, jet planes, the biotoxin Ricin used in Great Britain, and sodium cyanide, the chemical weapon used in the 1993 World Trade Center bombing.

Al Qaeda has additional options. Three years after the terrorist attacks of 9/11, U.S. Customs and Border Protection has identified ocean cargo containers as the prime vehicles for smuggling weapons of mass destruction (WMDs) into the United States. This year alone, ships will deliver more than 7 million cargo containers to America's seaports. The number will continue to grow. It has every year.

Steel-frame oceangoing containers come in 20- and 40-foot lengths, crammed with everything from furniture to parts for

General Motors, and they can weigh as much as 30 tons each. Each one also has the potential to contain a weapon of mass destruction that could be detonated when the ship reaches an American port or offloaded and transported to be detonated in one of our major cities.

Customs and Border Protection, the newly combined agency within the Department of Homeland Security, has stepped up inspections of incoming containers—from 2 percent to 4 percent of the total. Four percent of 7 million means 280,000 get inspected—and 6,720,000 do not. "We look at 100 percent of those that are high risk," says Jayson P. Ahern, who is the assistant commissioner, Office of Field Operations.

That is not a comforting thought. According to the Navy League,

> Containers already have been used by terrorists. In 1998, a vessel controlled by al Qaeda brought the explosives into Mombassa that were used to bomb the U.S. embassies in Kenya and Tanzania. More recently there was the "terrorist in a box" incident—in October 2001, when a container destined for Toronto was opened by suspicious authorities during a port stop in Italy. Inside was a suspected al Qaeda member who had fitted the container with all of the necessities of daily living as well as a variety of forged documents, electronics equipment, and blueprints and floor plans of various "sensitive" facilities throughout North America.

At the U.S. Senate Governmental Affairs Committee hearing in 2003 on the threat potential of cargo containers, Under Secretary of the Border and Transportation Security Directorate for the Department of Homeland Security Asa Hutchinson told Congress, "Ocean-going sea containers represent the most important artery of global commerce—some 48 million full sea cargo containers move between the world's major seaports each year, and nearly 50 percent of all U.S. imports (by value) arrive via sea containers." Pat Jones, spokesman for the Customs and Border Protection, gave me an estimate of more than 7 million cargo containers arriving at U.S. seaports annually.

"Because of the sheer volume of sea-container traffic and the opportunities it presents for terrorists, containerized shipping is uniquely vulnerable to terrorist attack. Most experts believe that a terrorist attack using a container as a weapon or as a means to smuggle a terrorist weapon, possibly a weapon of mass destruction, is likely. If terrorists used a sea container to conceal a weapon of mass destruction and detonated it on arrival at a port, the impact on global trade and the global economy could be immediate and devastating—all nations would be affected."[1]

Over the years, al Qaeda has become more than itself. It is a "state of mind" that can give rise to the "lone wolf" terrorist who suddenly adopts the al Qaeda philosophy of Jihad, for reasons of his own. That kind of terrorist is even harder to predict than the card-carrying member because he will give almost no warning of his intent. Al Qaeda's most dangerous feature is this predisposition to be brought into Militant Islam that can be trigged by exposure to something in a mosque, or on the Internet, or through media coverage of an event.

I'd grown used to seeing warnings ignored. At that briefing in Washington where they joked about Pat Robertson and Jerry Falwell, I saw *why* they were ignored. My hosts were hung up on the graying secular terrorists of the past, not the al Qaeda I knew that could explode without notice. One assured me, "Significant inroads have been made into damaging al Qaeda. This is proved by the fact there hasn't been another 9/11-type attack." I asked him if he was familiar with the tale of the Bedouin chief who waited forty years to avenge a personal insult—and friends wanted to know why the chief had been in such a rush.

Most troubling was their general agreement that Israel was the cause of America's problems with al Qaeda. Blaming the Arab-Israeli conflict on Israel alone ignored the fact that a Muslim collective does exist, that Muslims do confer, and that the Muslim world must be held accountable for its actions—actions that make it clear that they have never given up on their fifty-year war to destroy Israel completely. In that conference room, the sympathies were clear. They could have taken turns chanting the mantra, "You have to understand the Arab position." Having lived or served in the Middle East, they "understood" the people, but that smug "insider" feeling only narrowed their perception.

I had hoped the briefing would show me that the experts were leading this country it in the right direction. They weren't.

Unfortunately, terrorism is a growth field. Demand for information is high, but too many "experts" are the kind that Colin Powell observed, often possessing more "data than judgment."

I knew one who right after 9/11 bought as many books on terrorism as he could find so he could answer questions as a terrorism expert on cable TV shows. He now runs a university center that studies terrorism.

In most cases, tasking the old guard to do a new job simply won't work. We need a government-funded national effort in America to create credential programs for a new breed of terrorism, and counterterrorism experts who will buttress law-enforcement agencies on the federal, state, and local levels.

There is precedent. The 1960s were a period marked by drug abuse, urban violence, draft-card burning, flag desecration, and racial tensions. Taking the lead, President Lyndon B. Johnson formed the National Advisory Commission on Civil Disorders. The commission took its name from the commission chairman, Illinois Governor Otto Kerner, and was driven in large part by the charismatic mayor of New York City, John V. Lindsay.

The Kerner Commission's first task was to determine what caused the 1967 race riots in cities such as New York and Los Angeles. It found that black Americans' frustration at the lack of economic opportunities as well as police insensitivity and misconduct played major roles in touching off urban violence. From the commission came the warning that America was in danger of becoming two societies, "separate and unequal."

In response, Congress enacted the 1968 Omnibus Crime Control and Safe Streets Act, which included the creation of the Law Enforcement Assistance Administration (LEAA) and the Law Enforcement Educational Program (LEEP). Both brought major changes to law-enforcement agencies. LEAA established grant programs for the purchasing of new equipment, hiring new personnel, and retraining older ones. Hostage negotiators, negotiating techniques, and more humane methods of crowd control were just some of the outcomes. LEEP afforded law-enforcement professionals the financial wherewithal to attend classes and spurred the growth of criminal-justice programs across the nation almost overnight.

The legislation allowed universities to get involved in law enforcement, infusing the system with progressive ideologies and academic analysis. The fusion developed modern theories and techniques of law enforcement used to this day. It allowed returning Vietnam veterans as well as minorities to enroll in criminal-justice programs leading to jobs in law enforcement.

It also gave America tools to deal with domestic crime as well as a new sensitivity to race, gender, and economic status; created a system for ensuring victims' rights; and spearheaded judicial recourse for individuals who were treated unfairly or whose civil rights were denied.

Yet terrorism is currently studied as part of the curriculum of many disciplines, including criminal justice, history, sociology, political science, and psychology—and each one believes the subject is best understood from its own perspective. That has encouraged myopia and a lack of innovative ideas. The right way to develop a cadre of well-trained individuals to address the problem of terrorism in America is compiling a complete body of knowledge within one department, preferentially on the doctoral level of a university graduate school.

The criminal-justice model has had success and must be applied to terrorism and counterterrorism programs. Experience tells us that counterterrorism justice programs would have the same salutary effect on the Muslim community as criminal-justice programs had on black communities. Muslim students would bring an understanding of religious and cultural differences, creating additional means to address grievances and secularize the larger community. Counterterrorism programs would also stimulate new thinking by attracting new talent. This, in turn, would foster new approaches.

Effective efforts in counterterrorism on the home front must center on understanding the terrorist's language, culture, history, methods, and psychology. It must connect to intelligence agencies and law-enforcement agencies. We can't use military personnel or apply the techniques used to kill terrorists in Iraq and Afghanistan to America, even if we wanted to. The Posse Comitatus Act precludes the military from involvement in domestic law enforcement.

Terrorism is too important to leave to people who found they could buy books and become instant experts. Nor should we roll tanks down our city streets. Rooting out terrorists will require an entirely different effort, one that must be studied and analyzed by the best minds this nation has to offer.

Israeli General Meir Amit is one of the greatest spies in the history of the intelligence community. As chief of the Mossad, Amit pulled off stunning coups, like stealing a Soviet MiG-21 right off an Iraqi airstrip. He is also widely known for relying first and foremost on human sources rather than electronic ones—HUMINT rather than SIGINT. Amit said, "You can get information by satellites, long-range cameras, and all kinds of electronic intelligence. You can use it to locate and to listen to telephone conversations, but mainly what we call HUMINT must be involved. Human intelligence can tell you what is going to happen."[2]

Amit stressed the need for detail: "You have to have a list of people, of suspects, whom you collect, people who are more dangerous, less dangerous, the operators, the executives, the helpers, and who have influence. You keep files and you know. You have to have a picture of exactly what is going on in the field. My point is you have to have a picture of who is who and the rules of the game."[3]

Many of the human intelligence sources America needs are already available. With very little retraining or adaptation, they can provide the street-level intelligence we need to find the terrorists among us.

Raw "product" is critical to the American intelligence agencies charged with locating the terrorists among us. Simply put, you cannot analyze data without data to analyze.

Even more is possible within a framework of real cooperation of the FBI, the CIA, and Homeland Security. A remarkable array of sources can be developed from members of federal agencies inside local communities, like the Federal Department of Probation, whose officers are vetted by the FBI itself for security clearance to be hired. The kind of intelligence described by Meir Amit is available right now, without retooling agents or combining thousands of people and scores of federal agencies at a cost of billions of dollars (see the appendix).

Finally, there is the Buddhist parable of three blind men asked to describe an object by touch. It is an elephant, but the blind man holding the tail says it's a snake, the man holding the trunk says it's a giraffe, and the one holding the leg says it's a tree stump. None could assemble the "whole" from its separate "pieces." In the same way, it's time we stopped allowing the whole of Islam's Holy War on America to be described by politicians, journalists, and others familiar with only part of it.

The only explanation as to why we continue to ignore the secret Islamic terror network in America is that the demands of political correctness have made us so afraid of being branded racists that we force ourselves to be color blind, identity blind, and gender blind till we end up, quite simply, totally blind.

The rules changed on 9/11. It was Militant Islam's signal that from that day on, all weapons of terror, including weapons of mass destruction, could and would be used, and that the fight is to the death. America cannot wait for Militant Islam to secure itself from what will surely be our massive reaction to their next attack.

This is what we have to do: Stop fighting the Holy War with a Cold War mentality; stop our enemy from using our constitutional rights to shield itself; launch a congressional investigation into the $1.5 billion khat trade in America; make sure that none of the 7 million ocean cargo containers coming to the

United States contains a weapon of mass destruction; and hold our elected officials to one simple unambiguous standard—results.

For those who lost loved ones in the tragic events of 9/11, take some consolation in the knowledge that their sacrifice was not in vain. Had 9/11 not alerted America to the terrorists within it, had we waited just a few more years, the secret Islamic terror network would have reached its goal: America riddled with a fully operational terrorist infrastructure, an environment where Islamic network agents' homes held nuclear and biological weapons instead of guns, and enough radical Muslim operatives and traitors to undermine this country from within—and they may be closer to it than we think.

We hope a terrorist attack won't happen again—that we'll never have to go through *anything* like 9/11 again. Yet, we've let down our guard in the years since 9/11. We can't let the memory of that day fade—it must be always be present to strengthen our resolve.

The Holy War on our home front is the first war in almost two centuries that America will have to fight on its own soil.

The weapons of war will be different, but it is war nonetheless.

DOCUMENTS

Document Set 1

The U.S. Department of Probation has enough on its hands with American criminals, but it also has to supervise foreigners with admitted ties to terrorist organizations. Here is a post–September 11 internal confidential memo from the supervising probation officer of "KM" and documentation from his case file.

MEMO

Date: April 4, 2002

To: ██████████USPO
██████████c, SUSPO

From: ██████████Supervising U.S. Probation Officer

Re: **FIST Status Report**██████████████████

Investigation of this case commenced on February 27, 2002 based upon a list of referrals provided FIST by Deputy Chief U.S. Probation Officer

Field and intelligence since February 27, 2002 discloses the following:

1. ██████████ operates a ██████ van, New York State license plate number

2. Confidential source information discloses that ██████████ was a member of the **AMAL Lebanese Group**. ██████████ utilized businesses to launder money through business accounts. Money forwarded to South America and then to Lebanon.

3. ██████████ overheard speaking Spanish by FIST.

4. ██████████ is a ██████ relative of ██████████ presently on supervision to USPO ██████████ prosecuted in EDNY for attempt to smuggle money out of the United States.

5. ██████████ frequents the ██████ **Deli**, Queens, NY. During surveillance, ██████████ is observed handing a small white letter size envelope to an individual believed to be ██████████. Also present at the meeting is ██████ These individuals arrived in a vehicle ██████████ leasing company. Vehicle is registered to ██████████ Astoria, NY. ██████████ maintains a State of ██████████ drivers license.

6.   also frequents   Jackson Heights, Queens.
NY, a store identified as
The owner of this business is |

7.   observed in conversation with individual
believed to be   is identified as source of
money which   attempted to smuggle out of the
United States   and
                    frequent same
                        observed speaking to .   at this

8.   frequents
Queens, NY, although reporting his address as :
Queens, NY. His name appears on the mailbox of Apartment   at the
address   listed his address on INS
documents as   presently resides at
                    Queens, NY.

Blank checks observed in   . reported residence in the name of
                        . entered the U.S. on two different occasions utilizing
Lebanese passports with different passport numbers.   isted his
address on INS documents as   also listed this
            address on INS documents.

9.   listed his address on INS documents as
                        Queens, NY.   (aka,
on supervision to SDNY and co-defendant of   listed his address in
the past as

10.   .   utilized Lebanese passports with two different
passport numbers to enter the U.S.

                                made   deposits during ·   and
        at .   **Bank** in NYC. He was not prosecuted.   observed in
company of female unsub looking at documents and various checks in a parked
motor vehicle. He is later observed meeting with unsub at Middle Eastern
restaurant for approximately 5 minutes. It is suspected that there was an exchange
of documents at the meeting.

11.　　　　　　　along with　　　　　　　　　　　　　　　　operate two
stores
During surveillances very little to almost no customer activity noted.

12.　　　　　　　　　sustained an arrest and conviction pre-federal offense for Grand
Larceny (attempted to use a fraudulent　　　　　device). He obtained U.S. Citizenship
while pending this felony case. ·It is unknown if.　　　　　　　reported this pending
arrest to INS. Decertification is possible if　　　　　　failed to report this
pending arrest.

13. Most recently　　　　　　　　　　　... .　　　　　, was held by local
authorities for shoplifting.　　　　　　　　　provided identification to police in the form of
his drivers license disclosing his home address inconsistent with his reported address,
specifically,　　　　　　　　　　　　　Queens, NY.

Equifax report for I　　　　　　　　　　and I　　　　　　　disclose numerous
and extensive lines of credit with zero balances. Both maintain checking accounts
with minimal deposits and balances and both report meager earnings. I
　　　　　　　　　　　. Both identified by U.S. Intelligence sources as linked to
extremists groups. Their style of living is consistent with extremist groups.

　　　　　　　discloses that　　　　　　　　　　　is owner of
　　　　　　　　　　　　　　Dun & Bradstreet lists the owner of
　　　　　　　　　　　　· Total assets for
$54,912. Sales for January 2001 through August 2001, $281,483. Cost of goods
$169,134. Gross profits, $112,349, expenses, $70,323, net income, $33,201.

-4-

Analysis of Intelligence Data

1.   has two Lebanese passports,
#
#

2.   , also has two Lebanese passports,
#
#

         was found to be in possession of l   checking account in September 2001.

3. Regarding   Queens, the following individuals are known to frequent this location and reported the same on INS documents. This address could be a mail drop or safe house.

         on 12/20/00
         05/10/01

             Lebanese passport   on 03/16/97
               during 10/96 & 01/01
               during 09/96
     Lebanese passport   on 04/04/00
        during 01/99
    during 01/99

4. Regarding   Astoria
         gave this as his address during 07/98

is linked to this address when arrested during 09/98,
investigation during 09/96 and when identified with Middle Eastern extremists during 12/00.

5.
         is linked to this address on 04/28/99.
    s linked to this address on 02/13/99.

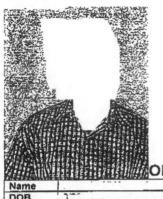

OFFENDER INTELLIGENCE REPORT

Name		POB	Lebanon
DOB		Weight	
Height		Status	Probation
Hair	Black	Expires	
Eyes	Brown	NYSID#	
FBI#		S.S. #	
INS#		Other	
DMV#		Other	

Reported Residence	Corona, NY,
Previous Addresses	
Home Telephone #	
Beeper/Cellular #	none reported
Other #'s	none reported
Reported Employment	The subject works in a warehouse
Work Telephone #	
Vehicles owned / driven	Chevy
AKA (s)	
Scars / Tatoos	none reported
Offense and related info	The subject was arrested by U.S. Customs at JFK airport on 12/4/00 and charged with Failure to file a currency report (ca agent . The subj attempted to leave the U.S. destined for Lebanon with $72,1 in money orders, checks and cash without filing a currency transaction report for these funds. The subject claimed that t funds were given to him by 12 different Middle Eastern partie be delivered to their alleged families.
Immigration Status	The subject entered the U.S. legally on a non-immigrant visa valid from · through The subject has allegedly filed for Permanent Residence based on his marriage. (Pend INS verification) It is noted that the subject is separated with wife, ' On 10-23-01, INS issued the subject an Employment Authorization Card.

Financial Information	An Equifax Credit report reveals the subject has 12 active lir of credit with a limit of $22040. The subject reports total mo income of $1600 in cash earnings. The subject reports that has been working in the United States since 1992, however. has never filed a tax return. The subject may have opened additional 16 lines of credit under the name of (SS# with a limit of $33796. This matter is pe investigation.

RELATED INDIVIDUALS

The following individuals signed sworn affadavits claiming ownership of the monies recovered during the subject's instant offense:

		Astoria, NY 11103	$6100
		Maspeth, NY 11378	$8200
		NY, NY 10040	$4000
		Brooklyn, NY 11220	$5000
		Flushing, NY 11365	$12400
		Astoria, NY 11103	$6300
		Astoria, NY 11103	$2200
		Elmhurst, NY 11370	$1578
		NY 11373	$1600
		Astoria, NY 11105	$4800
		Astoria, NY 11105	$4200
		Brooklyn, NY 11211	$3000

A search of the subject's apartment revealed that the subject was in possession of various credit card statements and personal checking accounts under the name of:

	Astoria, NY	Public Record Searches reveal this address to be a mail receiving service.
	Elmhurst, NY	Address also used by subject
		Address also used by subject

REPLY TO:
USPO

FIELD INVESTIGATION SERVICES AND SURVEILLANCE
TEAM REFERRAL REPORT

NAME		POB	Lebanon
DOB		FBI #	
HEIGHT		INS #	
WEIGHT	16s	NYSID #	
EYE COLOR	Brown	DMV #	
HAIR COLOR	Black	SS #	
RACE	White	OTHER	lacts#
STATUS	Supervised Release	OTHER	
T/D			

RESIDENCE

LIC, N.y

(718)

RESIDENCE OCCUPANTS
Names, Relation,
DOB, Description

ny

unemployed

OTHER KNOWN
RESIDENCES

LIC, Ny 11103

176

L

048 EQUIFAX CREDIT INFORMATION SERVICES,   P O BOX 740241,
  - 1150 LAKE HEARN DRIVE STE 460,ATLANTA,GA,30374-0241,800/

                SINCE 01/04/94 FAD 11/30/00   FN-247
                              ,11103,TAPE RPTD 03/00
                              ,11103,DAT RPTD 10/99
                        ,11103,DAT RPTD 10/99

i-01/94-12/00,PR/OI-NO,FB-NO, ACCTS:21,HC$0-15100, 2-ZEROS, 18-ONES, 1-OTHER

S-HBNA NV CT	11/30/	ATT-UCS	03/02/
CAPONE	10/14/	CITICRPDC	05/05/
BKONE	04/20/	US PROBATN	03/10/
ASSOC NATL	02/13/	FIRST USA	01/29/
FIRST USA	01/23/	BK1ST CARD	01/19/

FIRM/ID CODE	RPTD	OPND	H/C	TRM	BAL	P/D	CS	MR	ECOA	ACCOUNT NUMBER
	12/00	05/99	80		0		O1	18	I	
REDIT CARD										
	11/00	07/95	15K		0		R1	27	I	
REDIT CARD										
		CREDIT	LIMIT							
:	12/00	07/95	12K		0		R1	65	I	
MOUNT IN H/C COLUMN IS CREDIT LIMIT										
	.1/00	10/00	5600		0		R1	01	I	
REDIT CARD										
MOUNT IN H/C COLUMN IS CREDIT LIMIT										
	11/00	02/98	1400		0		R1	33	I	
EDIT CARD										
MOUNT IN H/C COLUMN IS CREDIT LIMIT										
	11/00	10/00	2000		0		R0		I	
NE OF CREDIT										
OUNT IN H/C COLUMN IS CREDIT LIMIT										
	12/00	05/98	1400		0		R1	31	I	
EDIT CARD										
OUNT IN H/C COLUMN IS CREDIT LIMIT										
	/00	09/95	15K		0		R1	63	I	
EDIT CARD										
DUNT IN H/C COLUMN IS CREDIT LIMIT										
	12/00	09/00	39		0		R1	03	I	
EDIT CARD										
	11/00	03/94	·13K		0		R1	74	I	DLA 07/98
	05/95-R2									
DUNT IN H/C COLUMN IS CREDIT LIMIT										
	10/98	5000			0		R1	25	I	
DUNT IN H/C COLUMN IS CREDIT LIMIT										
	10/00	09/96	11K	10	0		R1	49	J	
DIT CARD										
UNT IN H/C COLUMN IS CREDIT LIMIT										
	10/00	01/94	12K		0		R1	72	J	
DIT CARD										
UNT IN H/C COLUMN IS CREDIT LIMIT										
	12/00	12/97	8000		0		R1	29	I	
DIT CARD										
UNT IN H/C COLUMN IS CREDIT LIMIT										
	1/00	07/99	7500		0		R1	16	I	

Document Set 2

Here are letters from my sources, one in the INS, and two in the U.S. District Court system, both telling me that they have interaction with known and suspected terrorists! It boggles the mind that our system knows there are terrorists walking around inside U.S. borders.

**U.S. Department of Justice**
Immigration and Naturalization Service
New York Office of Asylum
One Cross Island Plaza
Rosedale, New York 11422

May 9, 2002

Professor Harvey W. Kushner

Re: Training for Asylum Staff

Dear Dr. Kushner:

Many of our applicants testify to having committed terrorist acts. Sometimes we have reason to believe they committed such acts even when they do not so testify. The information you provided will be valuable in interviewing such asylum applicants.

Thanking you again for helping us in our work, I am

Sincerely,

Director

UNITED STATES DISTRICT COURT
EASTERN DISTRICT OF NEW YORK

CHIEF U.S. PROBATION OFFICER

UNIONDALE, N.Y.

76 CLINTON STREET, ROOM 405
BROOKLYN, NY 11201
718-330-2828

U. S. COURTHOUSE
2 UNIONDALE AVENUE
UNIONDALE, NY 11553-1258
516-485-7140

U.S. COURTHOUSE
300 RABRO DRIVE
HAUPPAUGE, NY 11788
516-582-1105

Dr. Harvey Kushner

Dear Dr. Kushner:

  Additionally, our officers occasionally supervise both known or suspected terrorists who are on parole or probation.

    You are a highly respected expert in the field

    Very truly yours,

    Chief Deputy U. S. Probation Officer

UNITED STATES DISTRICT COURT
EASTERN DISTRICT OF NEW YORK
PROBATION OFFICE

CHIEF PROBATION OFFICER

75 CLINTON STREET, ROOM 4
BROOKLYN 11201-4201
718-330-2626

U.S. COURTHOUSE
2 UNIONDALE AVENUE
UNIONDALE, NY 11553-1251
516-485-7140

U.S. COURTHOUSE
300 RABRO DRIVE
HAUPPAUGE 11788
516-882-1105

BROOKLYN, NEW YORK

Dr. Harvey Kushner

Dear Dr. Kushner:

Your words are particularly haunting. Your warnings
certainly ring true

My officers deal with a wide range of offenders on a daily basis.
We are obligated to supervise suspected terrorists while they are
free in the community

Very truly yours,

Chief Deputy
U.S. Probation Officer

Document Set 3

Even a high-ranking Marine from headquarters in Quantico feels he isn't getting the help he needs to fight terrorism from inside his organization.

UNITED STATES MARINE CORPS
SECURITY BATTALION
MARINE CORPS BASE
MARINE CORPS COMBAT DEVELOPMENT COMMAND
QUANTICO, VIRGINIA 22134-5000

Dr. Harvey W. Kushner

Dear Dr. Kushner:

                I have found that there
is a lack of up to date information in the Marine Corps regarding terrorism, which has forced me
to go to outside sources to perform my duties.

Sincerely,

United States Marine Corps

Document Set 4

Here is part of the Department of Justice's translation of an organizational document found in 1981, when the secret Islamic terror network was first taking root in the United States. It is followed by our most recent expert translation and the handwritten Arabic original.

Case #	: 265-CTP-39461
Source	: Residence-Box One
Date	: June, 1981
Translator	:
Translation	: Verbatim
Notes	: Translator's notes are in italic

In The Name Of God, The Most Compassionate, The Most Beneficent

CHARTER

Classification : Confidential
Date : Shaaban 1401
June 1981

(Two eyes the fire would not touch, an eye
that cried fearing Allah, and an eye that
stood guard for Allah) Hadith Sharif
(*Prophetic Tradition*)

The Center For Studies, Intelligence And Information (CSII)
(The Arabic acronym of the Center is DAM)

Contents

Title	Subject	Page
Article One	Introduction	1
Article Two	General Objectives of the Center	2
Article Three	The Organizational Structure of the Center	3
Article Four	The Tasks of the Divisions of the Center And their Organizational Structures	5
Article Five	Guidebook of CSII	9
Article Six	Validity of the Charter and its amendment	19
Addendum One	The Sections of the Department of Information	20
Addendum Two	The Keys of the Cipher	22
Addendum Three	The Information Apparatus	23
Addendum Four	The Investigations or the Intelligence	25
Addendum Five	The Documentation Dossier and The Monthly Information Dossier	31

(Note: The page numbers in this document do not correspond to the numbering in the original Arabic document)

EXHIBIT# 6 (10)

ADMITTED

Date

Immigration Judge

IN THE NAME OF ALLAH, MOST GRACIOUS, MOST MERCIFUL

PRAISE BE TO GOD, PRAYER AND PEACE UPON THE MESSENGER OF GOD

REGULATION OF THE CENTER FOR STUDIES, INTELLIGENCE AND INFORMATION (DAM)

Article One: Introduction

Sound planning, wise decisions, and rational political conduct require a certain amount of precise informations and an enlightened awareness of the course of events and their backgrounds as well as a clear vision and an ability to analyze, explain and connect events. That's why information has become a preoccupation for governments, political entities, economic establishments, the media and others.

Since the Movement works in a world of interconnected interests, multiple motives and complex motion, it must of necessity have a wealth of information and a sound perception of its environment and what goes on around it. Muslims, more than others, should be interested in the necessary information mediums since they read God's verse, (Do those who walk with their heads stooped down have a better guidance than those who walk upright on a straight path), having also an example in the life story of the revered Messenger, prayer and peace be upon him, which confirms that.

Furthermore, the unique position which characterize the Islamic movement in North America provides it with good opportunities for observation, monitoring and probing since we are in the heart of "civilization" focal point which impacts negatively or positively the orientations of culture and social change in the lands of the Islamic world. In addition, we are in the political center that leads the conspiracy against our Islamic world, and in the [lair] of Zionist and christianizing organizations as well as other entities like them which plan and work to undermine the foundations of Islam and the Islamic movement in our countries. We are also in a country that hosts all of the subservient parties, be they of the right or the left, that are active in our countries under different names and labels. From here we can monitor the directions of the American policy, and the movements of the suspect entities. We are able also to make a diagnosis of the diseases of civilization that are deemed as medicines and antidotes in our countries. All of this we shall put in the service of the Islamic calling everywhere.

Our young men are, thank God, well qualified in every discipline of knowledge, and they are located in different parts of the Islamic world. They are, hence, in a position that enables them to undertake this task. It would be absurd not to benefit from their potentials and abilities. It is, therefore, within our power to establish an advanced Center for Studies, Intelligence and Information which, with concerted efforts with our brethren in Islamic countries, would gather information, conduct studies, preserve and share them with our brethren in the concerned countries.

Article Two: General Objectives of the Center

1- Gathering of necessary information that would be used in planning the work of the calling and in the political follow-up.

2- Putting relevant information in the service of the Islamic work and the international Islamic movement.

3- Using appropriate information to provide protection for the Islamic movement.

4- preparation of advanced and modern scientific studies in various current affairs that are of concern to Islam and muslims in general, and the Islamic movement in particular.

5- guiding brothers in their specializations, and managing to benefit from them in serving the movement.

بسم الله الرحمن الرحيم

لائحة

مركز – حام –

تصنيف : خاص
التاريخ : شعبان ١٤٠١
حزيران ١٩٨١

(عينان لا تمسها النار
عين بكت من خشية الله
وعين باتت تحرس في سبيل الله)
حديث شريف

المحتويـــات

العنوان	الموضوع	الصفحة
البند الأول	مقدمة	١
البند الثاني	أوضاع الحركة والعصابة	٢
البند الثالث	الهيكل التنظيمي للمركز	٢
البند الرابع	مهمات شعب الدوريات وكلاً التنظيمية	٥
البند الخامس	دليل مركز حام	٩
البند السادس	سريان اللائحة وتبديلها	١٩
ملحق ١	تنظيم العدو في قسم العمليات	٢٠
ملحق ٢	مفاتيح كيماء الشيفرة	٢٢
ملحق ٣	الأجهزة اللازمة	٢٢
ملحق ٤	المباحث أو المخابرات	٢٥
ملحق ٥	الملف الوثائقي وبيان المعلومات الشهري	٢٦

بســم الله الرحمن الرحيم

الحمد لله والصلاة والسلام على رسول الله ...

لائحة مركز الدراسات والاستخبارات والمعلومات
(دام)

البند الأول

مقدمة –   إن التخطيط السليم والقرارات الحكيمة والسلوك السياسى
الرشيد يستلزم قدراً من المعلومات الدقيقة والإدراك
الواعى لمجريات الأمور وخلفياتها بموضوع الرؤية والقدرة
على تحليل الحوادث وتحليلى وربطها . لذلك فقد أصبحت
المعلومات تتأثر باهتمامات الكيانات والرؤيات السياسية
والمؤسسات الاقتصادية وأجهزة الإعلام وغيرها .
وحيث أن الحركة تعمل فى عالم متشابك المصالح متعدد
الدوافع معقد الحركة فلابد . أن يكون لديها أجهزة المعلومات
الدائرة والرصد الحثيث لما يحيط بها وتعمل مسئولوها
والمسلمون من أجرى بالاهتمام بمسائل المعلومات اللازمة
من منهج وهم يقربعم تول لهم نعالى دأ مندهيشه ملكا
ظلك وجعد أحدى أسمر ميشه سعيا على صراط مستقيم)
ولزم فى صدرى سيرة الرسول الكريم عليه الدعاء قدم ما ذكر ذلك .
كما أن الوضع الخطير الذى تشير به المرأة المسلمة
فى أمريكا الشمالية ما يستدعى لها منصبا جيدة للمراقبة والمتابعة
والرصد والاستحضان حمية أنها فى قلب لصورة "الحضارية"
والتى تؤشر سلبيا أمرا بجاباً فى اتجاهات لثقافة والتحول
الاجتماعى فى بلدى العالم الإسلامى . كما أننا فى مركز لتوجيه
السياسى الذى يقود الحوارات على ما لمنا للإصلاح ووضعنا
المنظمات العربوبنتر والتنصير وما شاكلها من صحيات
تخطيط وتعمل لتفويض دعائم الإسلام والرؤية الإسلامية لأراضينا .
ونحن أيضا لا بد يستهدفنا جميع لأحزاب لحميلة التى تنشط
فى بلادنا سيعيم وياستـمت مختلف لإصلاح وإشمالات .
ومن ضنا فلا ننا نلتقى أمر نرصد اتجاهات السياسة
الأمريكية وتركات الهيئات المشبوهة كما نلتقى أن
نتفحص لبلاغاً الحضارية التى تحمى فى بلادنا وردائنا
وتراثنا وضعنا كل ذلك فى حملة الدعوة الإسلامية كل مكان .
وان شيئنا والحمدلله شباب مؤهل فى كل مكان سيصحول
لمعرفة ونستقر إلى بمؤية مختلفة من أجزاء الإسلامى .

189

Document Set 5

A U.S. District Court document records the designs the secret Islamic terror network had on the entire country as early as the 1980s.

UNITED STATES DISTRICT COURT
MIDDLE DISTRICT OF FLORIDA
TAMPA DIVISION

UNITED STATES OF AMERICA
v.
SAMI AMIN AL-ARIAN
a/k/a "Amin,"
a/k/a "The Secretary,"
a/k/a "Abu Abdullah,"

(186) On or about November 20, 1995, in Tampa, Florida, SAMI AMIN
AL-ARIAN possessed, at his residence:

(1) A document entitled the "Charter of the Center of Studies, the
Intelligence and the Information," which set forth a detailed description of
the structure and operation of a hostile intelligence organization in the
United States and elsewhere. The document included the organizational
structure, duties, responsibilities, espionage methods and targets,
counterintelligence and precautionary measures, methods of reporting and a
cipher system to make the hostile intelligence organization appear to be
affiliated with a university;

----

*"In the Charter, on a separate sheet paper is the drawing of a map of the
United States and Canada divided into the four following sections:*

- *The Western Region with dots on the cities of San Francisco, Los Angeles,
  and Denver*
- *The Central Region with dots on Houston, New Orleans, St. Louis,
  Chicago, Indianapolis, and Detroit*
- *The Eastern Region with dots on Boston, New York, Philadelphia,
  Washington, Raleigh, and Miami*
- *The Canadian Region with dots on Toronto and Montreal*

(Also, the following is written under the drawing):
A demonstrative illustration of the location of the team of researchers.
(The Bureau of North America)"

"DRAWING OF A MAP"

"Charter of the Center of Studies, the Intelligence and the Information"

(On a separate sheet of paper is the drawing of a map of the United States and Canada divided into the four following sections):

- *The Western Region with dots on the cities of San Francisco, Los Angeles and Denver.*
- *The Central Region with dots on Houston, New Orleans, St. Louis, Chicago, Indianapolis and Detroit*
- *The Eastern Region with dots on Boston, New York, Philadelphia, Washington, Raleigh and Miami*
- *The Canadian Region with dots on Toronto and Montreal.*

(Also, the following is written under the drawing):
A demonstrative illustration of the location of the team of researchers.
(The Bureau of North America)

The Method Of Determination Of The Subjects Suggested For Study:

We are not in the process of the detailed determination of the subjects recommended for studies but light should be shed on the determination of some techniques concerning specifying these subjects:

1- The determination of the priorities and subjects up for discussion by the Shura Council and the Executive Offices in addition to the suggestions and the requirements of the brothers in the Levant. *(The Middle East)*
2- It is preferable that the subjects suggested for studies take the operational aspect, meaning that the study should have a realistic beneficial impact on the activity of the Group.
3- Listening to the suggestions of the brothers members of the departments, their opinions and their remarks on the suggested subjects so the interaction is accomplished between the Command and the base.

The Guidelines of the Departments in the Division

1- The Department of Educational Studies:
Developing studies and researches on the matters and concepts that the Islamic Action requires, or benefiting from available studies on the issues of the Holy Koran, the Hadith Sharif, the doctrine, the line of conduct, the ideology, the ethics, and the Arabic language and its literature, and that in coordination with the office of education. It also works on originating educational programs for various levels and programs for the centers of general activity such as the Muslim Arab Youth Association and the Center of Islamic Teaching. It may also list the parties and the Islamic personalities in America and the East and study the way to benefit from them, and works on finding links with the research and Fatwa centers in the *(Middle)* East.

12

Holy War: The Charter Map

This map, found in the Charter was created in the '80s.
Few, if any, terrorist groups were operating
in the cities shown on the map.
It is now 2004. Terrorist groups are operating
in <u>every</u> city shown on the map, but by far,
the largest presence is Hamas.

BOSTON
Al Qaeda
Hamas

NEW YORK
Al Qaeda
Al Muhajiroun
Gama'a al-Islamiyya
Hezbollah
Hamas
PLO
Fatah

PHILADELPHIA
Al Qaeda
Al Muhajiroun
Gama'a al-Islamiyya
Hezbollah
Hamas
PLO
Fatah

WASHINGTON D.C.
Hezbollah
Hamas
Al Qaeda
Palestinian Islamic Jihad

RALEIGH
Hamas
Palestinian Islamic Jihad

MIAMI
Hamas
Palestinian Islamic Jihad
Fatah
PLO

NEW ORLEANS
Hamas

DETROIT
Gama'a al-Islamiyya
Hezbollah
Hamas
PLO
Fatah

INDIANAPOLIS
Hamas

CINCINNATI
Hamas

ST. LOUIS
Abu Nidal

HOUSTON
Al Qaeda
Hamas
Muslim Brotherhood
Palestinian Islamic Jihad

DENVER
Hamas

SAN FRANCISCO
Al Qaeda
Hamas
Abu Sayyaf Group

LOS ANGELES
Hamas
Gama'a al-Islamiyya
Al Qaeda

Document Set 6

World Assembly for Muslim Youth sells such "educational" programming as *A Monkey Desecrates a Mosque,* shown below. Note that the box of the audio cassette features a Star of David and a caricature of a Jew.

THE FOLLOWING HATE-SPEECH TAPE
RAISES MONEY FOR WAMY and HAMAS

Translation: Front Cover (right side)

Title: A Monkey Desecrates A Mosque

Saad Al-Buraik

3 Saudi Riyals

Revenues from the sale of this tape go to our Muslim brothers in Palestine

Document Set 7

Law-enforcement officials know very little about khat, a very profitable narcotic coming into the United States from African countries with ties to the Islamic terrorist network. Because there's so little awareness of it, khat is often mistaken for a vegetable.

Khat Rolled In Newspaper For Transport

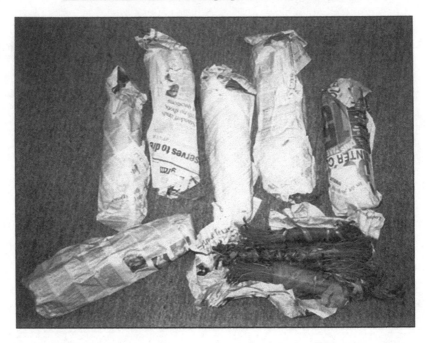

Khat must be transported quickly to market because it loses potency within 48 hours. It is often transported into the United States from Great Britain and Canada via package delivery services and by couriers on commercial aircraft. Khat also is transported into the United States from Canada by private vehicle. To maintain freshness, khat is wrapped in plastic bags, banana leaves, or newspapers and sprinkled with water.

These photographs are from the National Drug Intelligence Center, 319 Washington Street, 5th Floor, Johnstown, PA 15901.

Document Set 8

This Department of Probation document shows that community service at the Queens Botanical Garden was part of the sentence for this heroin-smuggling member of the secret Islamic terror network.

FIELD INVESTIGATION SERVICES AND SURVEILLANCE
TEAM REFERRAL REPORT

NAME		**POB**	
DOB		**FBI #**	
HEIGHT	'	**INS #**	
WEIGHT	lbs.	**NYSID #**	
EYE COLOR	Brown	**DMV #**	
HAIR COLOR	Brown	**SS #**	
RACE	White	**OTHER**	
STATUS	TSR	**OTHER**	AKA: Abraham
T/D			

RESIDENCE

Flushing, ny 11355

RESIDENCE OCCUPANTS
Names, Relation,
DOB, Description

**OTHER KNOWN
RESIDENCES**

Offense: Importation of heroin.

Sentence: (9/15/97) 30 months imprisonment, 3 years Supervised release, $100 Special assessment and 200 hours of c/s.

Current Sanctions.

CCC, HC, CS, Violence, Drug Use and Current Treatment, Mental Health and Current Treatment, Currently Investigated by Law Enforcement Agency, Pending Prosecutions, or Violations.

Ordered to perform 200 hours of C/S.
He was placed at The Queens Botanical Garden, however, he has not gone since
He has approximately 80 hours remaining.

NARRATIVE OF ACTIVITIES BY SUPERVISING OFFICER TO INVESTIGATE SUSPICIONS OR ALLEGATIONS

The subject requested permission to travel to Saudi Arabia

for religious purposes. He was denied permission, however, the dates he indicated he wanted to travel was from   to

He planned on flying

From   , flight #   @
Returning to   , flight #

NOTES

Chapter 1. Universities

1. Michael Isikoff, "Tensions in the FBI," msnbc.com, October 20, 2003, http://www.msnbc.com/news/980186.asp#ten.
2. Michael Isikoff and Mark Hosenball, "Reinstated," msnbc.com, February 25, 2004, http://msnbc.msn.com/id/4374015/.
3. Ibid.
4. Rahid Khalidi, "America Anointed," prospect.org, November 19, 2001, http://www.prospect.org/print/V12/20/khalidi-r.html.
5. Margaret Hunt Gram, "Professors Condemn War in Iraq at Teach-in," Columbia Spectator.com, March 27, 2003, http://www.columbiaspectator.com/vnews/display.v/ART/2003/03/27/3e82ec713097?in_archive=1.
6. "Sami Al-Arian, in his own words," sptimes.com, February 21, 2003, http://www.sptimes.com/2003/02/21/TampaBay/Sami_Al_Arian__in_his.shtml.
7. "Accused academic speaks out," news.bbc.com, February 26, 2003, http://news.bbc.co.uk/1/hi/uk/2802427.stm.
8. "How U.S. extremists fund terror," worldnetdaily.com, January 5, 2004, http://www.worldnetdaily.com/news/article.asp?ARTICLE ID=36441.
9. "Al-Arian rise in U.S. began in academics," sptimes.com, February 21, 2003, http://www.sptimes.com/2003/02/21/TampaBay/Al_Arian_s_rise_in_US.shtml.
10. "Palestinian Professor Accused of Aiding Terror Ordered Deported," islam.online, November 24, 2001, http://www.islam-online.net/english/News/2001-11/26/article9.shtml.
11. Robert Spencer, "Al-Arian: Terrorist Professor and His Campus Allies," frontpagemag.com, February 26, 2003, http://www.frontpagemag.com/Articles/ReadArticle.asp?ID=6306.
12. "Florida Professor Denies Terror Ties," cbsnews.com, August 22, 2002, http://www.cbsnews.com/stories/2003/02/20/attack/main541290.shtml.

13. Graham Brink, "Lawsuits Raise Stakes for Opponents" sptimes.com, August 22, 2002, http://www.sptimes.com/2002/08/22/TampaBay/Lawsuit_raises_stakes.shtml.

14. Anthony T. Brooks, "Statement of USF's Dismissal of Dr. Sami Al-Arian," http://216.239.41.104/search?q=cache:wKeuTZH9FcUJ:www.academicfreespeech.com/los_brooks.html+Anthony+T.+Brooks&hl=en&ie=UTF-8.

15. Ibid.

16. "Remarks by Dr. Sami A. Al-Arian address to the University of South Florida Faculty Senate," myaol.aol.com, January 9, 2002, http://myaol.aol.com/stories/inedex.psp?cp=myfresh.

17. "Sami Al-Arian, in his own words," op. cit.

Chapter 2. Charities

1. Evan McCormick, "Jihad in America," frontpagemagazine.com, September 5, 2003, http://www.frontpagemag.com/Articles/ReadArticle.asp?ID=9706.

2. Ibid.

3. "Kirk Campaign Employed Anti-Israel Activist," austireview.com, June 7, 2002, http://www.austinreview.com/articles/2002_04b/kirk.htm.

4. "Statement of Secretary Paul O'Neill on the Blocking of Hamas Financiers' Assets," U.S. Treasury Department, Office of Public Affairs, December 4, 2001, http://www.ustreas.gov/press/releases/po837.htm.

5. Joe Kaufman, "The CAIR-Terror Connection," frontpagemag.com, April 29, 2004, http://www.frontpagemag.com/Articles/ReadArticle.asp?ID=13175.

6. Evan McCormick, op. cit.

7. Evan McCormick, op. cit.

8. Michael C. Kotzin, "Terrorism Today and the Chicago Connection," juf.org, September 28, 2001, http://www.juf.org/news_public_affairs/articles.asp?key=2626.

9. Ibid.

10. Tom Jackman and Spencer S. Hsu, "Moran to Break with Muslim Activist," washingtonpost.com, February 2, 2002, http://www.juf.org/news_public_affairs/article.asp?key=2626.

11. Ibid.

12. J. Michael Waller, "Alamoudi Received Cash from Libyan 'Jihad Fund,' " insightmag.com, October 13, 2003, http://www.insightmag.com/main.cfm?include=detail&storyid=525875.

13. Ibid.

14. Ibid.

15. Ibid.

16. "United States of America v. Abdulrahman M. Alamoudi," newsfindlaw.com, October 23, 2003, http://news.findlaw.com/hdocs/docs/terrorism/usalamoudi102303.pdf.

17. Eric Lichtblau, "Islamic Leader to Plead Guilty in Libya Plot," eri24.com, July 30, 2004, http://eri24.com/news6714.htm.
18. Jerry Seper, "American Muslim leader arrested," washingtontimes.com, September 30, 2003, http://www.washtimes.com/national/20039030-120014-1161r.htm.
19. Ibid.
20. "Subversion from Within: Saudi Funding of Islamic Extremist Groups in the United States," washingtoninstitute.org, October 2, 2003, http://www.washingtoninstitute.org/watch/policywatch/policywatch2003/790.htm.
21. J. Michael Walker, "The American Muslim Council in Its Own Words," insightmag.com, March 4, 2003, http://www.insightmag.com/main.cfm?include=detail&storyid=384362.
22. Kenneth R. Timmerman, "Exclusive: Controversial Professor Arrested in Florida was White House Guest," insightmag.com, February 21, 2003, http://www.insightmag.com/news/2003/03/04/National/Exclusive.Controversial.Professor.Arrested.In.Florida.Was.White.House.Guest-376498.shtml.
23. "Muslim Chaplain Sent to Guantanamo," BaptistStandard.com, January 28, 2002, http://www.baptiststandard.com/2002/1_28/pages/muslim_chaplain.html.

Chapter 3. The Prison System

1. "Press Release," February 6, 2003, www.state.ny.us/governor.
2. "Saudi Time Bomb?" *Frontline*, 2001, http://www.pbs.org/wgbh/pages/frontline/shows/saudi/.
3. Stephen Schwartz, *Two Faces of Islam: The House of Sa'ud from Tradition to Terror* (New York: Doubleday, 2002).
4. Chuck Colson, "Evangelizing for evil in our prisons: Radical Islamists seek to turn criminals into terrorists," opinionjournal.com, June 24, 2002, www.opinionjournal.com/editorial/feature.html?id=110001885.
5. John S. Pistole, Assistant Director of the FBI Counterterrorism Division, Statement for the Record Before the Subcommittee on Terrorism, Technology, and Homeland Security of the Senate Judiciary Committee, October 14, 2003, http://judiciary.senate.gov/testimony.cfm?id=960&wit_id=2718.
6. Department of Justice, Office of the Inspector General, "A Review of the Bureau of Prisons' Selection of Muslim Religious Services Providers," April 2004, www.usdoj.gov/oig/igspecrl.htm.
7. www.bethlehemforpeace.org.
8. Bill Berkowitz, "Painting homeland terrorism black," workingforchange.com, April 25, 2003, http://www.workingforchange.com/article.cfm?ItemID=14896.
9. "Government Plans to Hold 'Dirty Bomber' Indefinitely," foxnews.com, June 14, 2002, http://www.foxnews.com/story/0,2933,55282,00.html.
10. Gail Russell Chaddock, "U.S. notches world's highest incarceration rate: A re-

port highlights extent to which many citizens have served time in prison," csmonitor.com, August 18, 2002, www.csmonitor.com/2003/0818/p02s01-usju.htm.

11. Frantz Fanon, *The Wretched of the Earth* (New York: Grove Press, 1965).

12. "Converts: Conversions in U.S. Prisons," mediaguidetoislam.sfsu.edu, http://mediaguidetoislam.sfsu.edu/intheus/06c converts.htm.

13. Ibid.

14. Department of Justice, Office of the Inspector General, op. cit.

15. Ibid.

16. Ibid.

17. Ibid.

18. Ibid.

19. Ibid.

20. Ibid.

21. Ibid.

22. Ibid.

23. Evan McCormick, "Pentagon Madrassas," frontpagemag.com, December 2, 2003, http://www.frontpagemag.com/Articles/ReadArticle.asp?ID=11063.

24. "Terror-Linked Group May Supply Muslim US Military Chaplains," usgovinfo.about.com, September 26, 2003, http://usgovinfo.about.com/b/a/029839.htm.

25. Mary Jacoby, "Muslim Linked to Al-Arian Trained Military Chaplins (Schumer Calls for Pentagon Investigation)," freerepublic.com, March 27, 2003, http://www.freerepublic.com/focus.f-news/877868/posts.

26. J. Michael Waller, "Alamoudi and Those Bags of Libyan Cash," insightmag.com, October 13, 2003, http://www.insightmag.com/main.cfm?include=detail&storyid=525860.

27. Kate O'Beirne, "The Chaplain Problem: What gives with imams in the military?—and others," nationalreview.com, October 27, 2003, http://www.findarticles.com/p/articles/mi_m1282/is_20_55/ai_108892926.

28. "American al-Qaeda Suspect's Imam Headed Probed Group," jihadwatch.org, May 30, 2004, http://www.jihadwatch.org/archives/2004_05.php.s

29. "Former Renton Student Held in Terrorism Probe," komotv.com, March 24, 2003, http://www.komotv.com/yourmoney/story.asp?ID=23821.

30. Nora Doyle, "Lindbergh Grad Connected to Terrorism," kingcountyjournal.com, March 18, 2003, http://www.kingcountyjournal.com/sited/story/html.124766.

31. Steven Emerson, *American Jihad: The Terrorists Living Among Us* (New York: Free Press, 2003).

32. Department of Justice, Office of the Inspector General, op. cit.

Chapter 4. Mosques

1. "Egypt: Land of Denial," newyorkwired.com, October 29, 2001, http://www. newyorkwired.com/editorial-10.29.01.htm.
2. Gersh Kuntzman, "What Would Jesus Do About Bin Laden?," skfriends.com, December 22, 2001, http://www.skfriends.com/wtc-what-would-jesus-do.htm.
3. Charles Schumer, "Saudis Playing Role in Spreading Main Terror Influence in United States," http://schumer.senate.gov/SchumerWebsite/pressroom/press_ releases/PR02009.pf.html.
4. David Harris, Hearing on "Palestinian Education: Teaching Peace and War," Senate Appropriations Committee, Subcommittee on Labor, Health and Human Services, and Education, October 23, 2003, http://www.ajc.org/Terrorism/ TestimonyDetail.asp?did=224&pid=1989.
5. American Jewish Committee, "The West, Christians and Jews in Saudi Arabian Schoolbooks-Abridged Version," http://www.ajc.org/InTheMedia/Publications Print.asp?did=750.
6. Ibid.
7. Ibid.
8. Ibid.
9. Larry Cohler-Esses, "Sowing seeds of hatred: Islamic textbooks scapegoat Jews and Christians," nydailynews.com, March 30, 2003, http://www.mydailynews. com/news/local/story/71199p-66134c.html.
10. Ibid.
11. Ibid.
12. Kenneth Adelman, "U.S. Islamic Schools Teaching Homegrown Hate," fox news.com, February 27, 2002, http://www.foxnews.com/story/0,2933,46610,00. html.
13. The Saudi Institute, "Saudis Spread Hate Speech in U.S.," Washington, D.C., September 2002, http://www.saudiinstitute.org.hate.htm.
14. Ibid.
15. Michael Powell, "No Choice but Guilty," washingtonpost.com, July 29, 2003, http://www.washingtonpost.com/ac2/we-dyn?pagename+article&node=%content ID=A59245-2003Jul28&notFound=true.
16. Jim Redden, "Lawyers: Give Us Kariye Affidavit," portlandtribune.com, August 15, 2003, http://www.portlandtribune.com/archview.cgi?id=19688.
17. Jim Redden and Jannie Robbin, "Mosque Leader: Brothers' Plan Was 'Beyond Stupid,' " portlandtribune.com, September 19, 2003, http://www.portlandtribune .com/archview.cgi?id=20391.
18. Jason Williams and Andrew Bret, "World Comes to Atlantic Avenue," journalism. nyu.edu, July 15, 2003, http://journalism.nyu.edu/pubzone/streetlevel/atlanticave/ world/money.htm.

19. "Muslim Chaplin Barred from Counseling NYC Inmates Because Mosque Allegedly Linked to al-Qaida," freerepublic.com, March 21, 2003, http://www.freerepublic.com/focus.f-news/871461/posts.

20. "Feds Link Money Smuggler to Outlawed Muslim Charity," cnn.com, November 27, 2003, http://www.cnn.com/2003/LAW/11/27/money.smuggling.ap/.

21. "Is Saudi Arabia Strategic Threat: The Global Propagation of Violence," uscrif.gov, November 18, 2003, http://www.uscrif.gov/index.php3?scale=1024.

22. Provided by the Saudi Institute, 1900 L Street NW, Washington, D.C., 20036.

23. http://www.wamyusa.org and http://www.wamy.co.uk.

24. "Has Someone Been Sitting on the FBI?" bbc.co.uk, June 11, 2001, http://news.bbc.co.uk/1/hi/events/newsnight/1645527.stm.

25. Charles Schumer, "Letter to Attorney General Ashcroft," September 17, 2003, http://216.239.41.104/search?q=cache:arYaanPLpeIJ:www.senate.gov/~schumer/SchumerWebsite/pressroom/special_reports/Ashcroft%2520and%2520WAMY%25209.16.03.pdf+Schumer+Ashcroft+WAMY&hl=en&ie=UTF-8.

26. Susan Schmidt, "Spreading Saudi Fundamentalism in U.S., Network of Wahhabi Mosques, Schools, Web Sites Probed by FBI," washingtonpost.com, October 2, 2003, http://www.washingtonpost.com/ac2/wp-dyn/A31402-2003Oct1?language=printer.

27. "Projects of Pride to the Islamic People and Honorable Achievements based on the feelings of Responsibility towards the Nation and without any Expectations. Important Steps to Expand and Renovate the Holy Mosques. The Kingdoms' Illustrious Efforts in the Field of Establishing Centers, Mosques and Islamic Institutes," http://www.ain-al-yaqeen.com/issues/20030131/feat1en.htm.

28. "Motive a mystery in grenade attack," cnn.com, March 24, 2003, http://www.cnn.com/2003/LAW/03/24/101.attack.ap/

29. "Muslim American Politics After September 11: Transcript of the Center's Conversation with Ahmed H. al-Rahim," eppc.org, December 29, 2003, http://www.eppc.org/publications/pubID.1947/pub_detail.asp

30. William McGowan, *Coloring the News: How Crusading for Diversity Has Corrupted American Journalism* (San Francisco, CA: Encounter Books, 2001).

31. "Profile: Abu Hamza," news.bbc.co.uk, May 27, 2004, http://news.bbc.co.uk/1/hi/uk/3752517.stm.

32. Michael Taarnby, "Profiling Islamic Suicide Terrorists: A Research Report for the Danish Ministry of Justice," Centre for Cultural Research, University of Aarhus, Finlandsgade, 28, Denmark, November 27, 2003, http://64.233.161.104/search?q=cache:2TkYJl1VlxEJ:www.jm.dk/image.asp%3Fpage%3Dimage%26objno%3D71157+Taarnby+Profiling+Islamic&hl=en&ie+UTF-8.

Chapter 5. The Drug Connection

1. "Atty. Gen. Ashcroft Outlines Attack on Narco-Terrorists," useu.be, July 30, 2002, http://www.useu.be/Terrorism/USResponse/July3002AshcroftNarcoTerrorists. html.

2. Personal interview, date withheld for security purposes.

3. "Street Advisory" by the New York Office of Alcoholism and Substance Abuse Services, "What is Khat?" leda.lycaeum.org, 1993, http://leda.lycaeum.org/?ID=8658.

4. "Khat Becoming Prevalent Behind Wheel," ndaa-apri.org, Autumn 2003, http://www.ndaa=apri.org/publications/newsletters/apri_highlights_ntlc_autumn_2003.html.

5. "Use of drug Khat up in some cities," usatoday.com, 2003, http://www.usatoday.com/news/nation/2002-09-10-khat_x.htm.

6. "Some cities are seeing an increase in the use of illegal drug khat," hamarey.com, October 9, 2002, http://www.hamarey.com/index.php/article/articleview/816/1/4/.

7. Shaker al-Ashwal, "Qat in America," ycmentimes.com, January 12–18, 1998, http://www. ycmentimes.com/98/iss02/health.htm.

8. Stephanie V. Siek, "Khat Use Growing in Several U.S. Cities," nwaonline.net, September 11, 2002, http://216.239.39.104/search?q=ache:r397CxRwMGAJ:www. nwaonline.net/pdfarchive/2002/September/11/9-11-02%2520B5.pdf+Dan+Rogan+10+to+20+Khat=related+charges&hl=en&ie=UTF-8.

9. Ibid.

10. "Intelligence Bulletin: Khat (Catha edulis)," usdoj.gov, May 2003, http://www. usdoj.gov/ndic/pubs3/3920/.

11. Ibid.

12. Ibid.

13. Ibid.

14. Ibid.

15. "Some cities are seeing an increase in the use of illegal drug khat," op. cit.

16. "The Khat Smugglers," bbc.co.uk, October 13, 2003, http://www.bbc.co.uk/insideout/southeast/series4/khat_smuggling.shtml.

17. "Inside Out exposes Kent 'mules' scam," bbc.co.uk, October 10, 2003, http://www.bbc.co.uk/pressoffice/pressreleases/stories/2003/10_october/10/kent_mules.shtml.

18. "Drugs and Terrorism: A New Perspective," usdoj.gov, September 2002, http://www.usdoj.gov/dea/pubs/intel/02039/02039.html.

Chapter 6. Counterfeiting Rings

1. Timothy P. Trainer, Testimony before House of Representatives Committee on International Relations, "International/Global Intellectual Property Theft: Links to Terrorism and Terrorist Organizations," iacc.org, http://216.239.39.104/search?q=cache:jbZ2XVf6ChgJ:www.iacc.org/teampublish/uploads/Testimony8.pdf+White+Paper+International/Global+Intellectual&hl=en%start=1&ie=UTF-8.

2. James Q. Wilson and George L. Kelling, atlantic.com, March 1982, http://www.theatlantic.com/politics/crime/windows.htm

3. John Mintz and Douglas Farah, "Small Scams Probed for Terror Ties: Muslim, Arab Stores Monitored as Part of Post-Sept. 11 Inquiry," washingtonpost.com, August 12, 2001, http://www. washingtonpost.com/ac2/wp-dyn?pagename=article&node=&contentIld=A6565-2002Aug11&notFound=true

4. "Al-Qa'idah Trading in Fake Branded Goods," BBC Monitoring Reports, September 11, 2003, and Lenore Taylor, "Big Business Targets Terrorist Pirates," *Austrian Financial Review,* January 29, 2003, cited in Timothy P. Trainer, op. cit.

5. James Nurton, "Why Counterfeiting is Not So Harmless," Managing Intellectual Property, September 2002, cited in Timothy P. Trainer, op.cit.

6. Ibid.

7. Ibid.

8. John von Radowitz, "Fake Internet Goods 'Linked to Terrorists,' " Press Association, June 25, 2002, and "Fake Goods Linked with Terrorist Fund-Raising; Consumer Fraud," *Western Mail,* June 26, 2002, cited in Timothy P. Trainer, op. cit.

9. "Ringleader Gets Maximum Sentence in Scheme to Help Hezbollah," http://www.foxnews.com/story/0,2933,79909,00.html, cited in Timothy P. Trainer, op. cit.

10. Jeffrey Goldberg, "In the Party of God; Hezbollah Sets Up Operations in South America and the United States," *New Yorker,* October 28, 2002; Manuel Roig-Franzia, "N.C. Man Convicted of Aiding Hezbollah; Cigarette Smuggling Said to Fund Terror," *Washington Post,* June 22, 2002, cited in Timothy P. Trainer, op. cit.

11. Ibid.

12. Ibid.

13. Kathleen Millar, "Financing Terror, Profits from Counterfeit Goods Pay for Attacks," *U.S. Customs Today,* November 2002, cited in Timothy P. Trainer, op. cit.

14. William Glaberson, "6 Are Charged With Selling Millions of Counterfeit Marlboros," *New York Times,* February 21, 2003, cited in Timothy P. Trainer, op. cit.

15. John Mintz and Douglas Farah, "Small Scams Probed for Terror Ties," *Washington Post,* August 12, 2002, cited in Timothy P. Trainer, op. cit.

16. Justification Review of the Office Program Policy Analysis and Government Accountability Office of the Florida Legislature, "Counterfeit and Diverted Drugs Threaten Public Health and Waste State Dollars," Report No. 03–18, February 2003, cited in Timothy P. Trainer, op. cit.

17. Andy Vuong, "The High Price of Knockoffs, Counterfeiting and Terrorism," globaloptions.com, June 24, 2003, http:www.globaloptions.com/news_06-24-03.htm.

18. Katherine Macklem, "The Terror Crisis has Lit a Fire under Ottawa's Lagging Anti-laundering Effort," *MacLean's,* October 22, 2001, cited in Timothy P. Trainer, op. cit.

19. The Engineer, *Fighting the Fakers*, at 16 (April 26, 2002); Phillippe Broussard, "Dangerous Fakes," *World Press Review*, January 1999, cited in Timothy P. Trainer, op. cit.

20. Douglas Pasternak, "Knockoffs on the Pharmacy Shelf, Counterfeit Drugs are coming to America," *U.S. News & World Report*, June 11, 2001, cited in Timothy P. Trainer, op. cit.

21. Ridgely Ochs, "Sounding Alarm on Counterfeit Drugs, FDA Investigating Recent Fake Drug Cases," *Newsday*, June 12, 2002, cited in Timothy P. Trainer, op. cit.

22. "U.S. Officials Arrest Viagra Counterfeiters," *Scrip*, May 22, 2002, and Ridgely Ochs, "Sounding Alarm on Counterfeit Drugs, FDA Investigating Recent Fake Drug Cases," *Newsday*, June 12, 2002, cited in Timothy P. Trainer, op. cit.

23. "Thompson Should Block Surge in Knockoff Drugs," *Wisconsin State Journal*, June 22, 2001, cited in Timothy P. Trainer, op. cit.

24. "Seniors Group Sues Drug Makers," cbsnews.com, May 20, 2004, http://www.cbsnews.com/stories/2004/05/20/health/main618621.shtml.

25. Statement of William K. Hubbard, Associate Commissioner for Policy and Planning, Committee on Government Reform, U.S. House of Representatives Hearing on Internet Drug Sales, March 18, 2004, cited in Timothy P. Trainer, op. cit.

26. "Fugitive Who Sold Counterfeit Baby Formula Convicted of Federal Criminal Charges, Department of Justice" (Press Release) (August 9, 2002), cited in Timothy P. Trainer, op. cit.

27. Timothy P. Trainer, op. cit.

28. "55 Killed in Crash of Norwegian Plane, None aboard Survive as Craft Plunges into Sea near Denmark," *Los Angeles Times*, September 9, 1989, cited in Timothy P. Trainer, op. cit.

29. Billy Stern, "Warning! Bogus Parts Have Turned Up in Commercial Jets. Where's the FAA?" *Business Week*, June 10, 1996, cited in Timothy P. Trainer, op. cit.

30. Ibid.

31. George W. Abbott Jr. and Lee S. Sporn, Trademark Counterfeiting § 1.03[C][3] (2002), cited in Timothy P. Trainer, op. cit.

32. S. Rep. No. 98-526 at 4 (1984), reprinted in 1984 U.S.C.C.A.N. 3627, 3630-31, cited in Timothy P. Trainer, op. cit.

33. H. Rep. No. 104-556, 104th Cong., 2d Sess., Conference Report from the Judiciary Committee (1996), cited in Timothy P. Trainer, op. cit.

34. Henry Gilgoff, "Counterfeit: Rip-offs of Popular Products Victimize Both Consumers and Manufacturers," *Newsday*, August 27, 1995, cited in Timothy P. Trainer, op. cit.

35. "Colgate Warns People against Fake Toothpaste," *Austin American Statesman*, August 12, 1996, cited in Timothy P. Trainer, op. cit.

36. Henry G. Cisneros, "The 'Broken Window' Theory," pan.ci.seattle.wa.us., January 1995, http://www.pan.ci.seattle.wa.us/police/prevention/Tips/broken_window. htm.

Chapter 7. Media

1. "Texas Internet Firm's Accounts Frozen Due to Hamas Link," ict.org, September 28, 2001, http://www.ict.org.il/spotlight/det.cfm?id=682.
2. "Texas Islamic Group Busted by Feds," cbsnews.com, December 18, 2003, http://www.cbsnews.com/stories/2004/07/27/terror/main632121.shtml.
3. "Statement of Secretary Paul O'Neill on the Blocking of Hamas Financiers' Assets," December 4, 2001, http://www.ustreas.gov/press/releases/po837.htm.
4. U.S. Department of Justice, "Senior Leader of Hamas and Texas Computer Company Indicted for Conspiracy to Violate U.S. Ban on Financial Dealings with Terrorists," 4law.co.il, December 18, 2002, http://www.4law.co.il/L1.htm.
5. Ibid.
6. Ibid.
7. "Attorney General Transcript: News Conference with President Bush and Secretary O'Neill," usdoj.gov, December 4, 2001, http://www.usdoj.gov/ag/speeches/2001/1204newsconferencewithbush.htm.
8. David Koenig, "Muslim Group Protest FBI Raid of Internet Business Suspected of Terrorist Ties," list.mircoshaft.org, September 6, 2001, http://lists.microshaft. org/pipermail/dmca_discuss/2001-September/000184.html.
9. "Al-Jazeera Praises Kerry," newsmax.com, March 16, 2004, http://www.newsmax.com/archives/ic/2004/3/16/132854.shtml.
10. "Cheney warned al-Jazeera about bin Laden tapes," February 1, 2002, http://www. cnn.com/2002/us/02/01/Cheney.al.jazeera/.
11. Ibid.

Chapter 8. Profiling

1. Michael Taarnby, "Profiling Islamic Suicide Terrorists: A Research Report for the Danish Ministry of Justice," Center for Cultural Research University of Aarhus, Finlandsgade, 28, Denmark, November 27, 2003, http://64.233.161.104/ search?q=cache:2TkYJ11V1xEJ:www.jm.dk/image.asp%3Fpage%3Dimage% 26objno%3D71157+Michael+Taarnby+Profiling+Islamic&hl=en&ie=UTF-8.
2. Jason L. Riley, "Racial Profiling and Terrorism," facstaff.bucknell.edu, October 24, 2001, http://www.facstaff.bucknell.edu/pagana/mg312/racialprofiling.html.
3. Kareem Fahim, "The Moving Target: Profiles in Racism," amnestyusa.org, http:// www.amnestyusa.org/amnestynow/racial-profiling.html
4. Henry Weinstein, Michael Finnegan and Teresa Watanbe, "Racial Profiling Gains Support as Search Tactic," latimes.com, September 24, 2001, http://www. latimes.com/news/nationworld/nation/la-092401racial.story

5. Kareem Fahim, op. cit.
6. "Sanctioned Bias: Racial Profiling Since 9/11," aclu.org, February 2004, http://www.aclu.org/SafeandFree/SafeandFree.cfm?ID=15102&c=207.
7. Ibid.
8. Ibid.
9. "Wrong Then, Wrong Now: Racial Profiling Before and After September 11, 2001," civilrights.org, http://www.civilrights.org/publications/reports/racial_profiling/.
10. http://www.aclu.org/ImmigrantsRights/ImmigrantsRightsMain.cfm.
11. Curt Anderson, "Justice Department Issues First Guidelines Banning Racial Profiling," signonsandiego.com, June 17, 2003, http://www.signonsandiego.com/news/nation/20030617-1330-racialprofiling.html.
12. "Sanctioned Bias: Racial Profiling Since 9/11," op. cit.
13. "Justice Dept. issues first federal guidelines banning racial profiling," usatoday.com, June, 17, 2003, http://www.usatoday.com/news/washington/2003-06-11-racial-profiling_x.htm.
14. "The Department of Justice Racial Profiling Guidance Has Loopholes," civil-rights.org.staff, June 23, 2003, http://www.civilrights.org/issues/cj/details.cfm?id=14156.
15. "Statement of Raul Yzaguirre on the Department of Justice Racial Profiling Guidance," nclr.org, January 19, 2003, http://www.nclr.org/content/news/detail/2353.
16. "DOJ's Guidance on the Misuse of Race and Ethnicity by Federal Law Enforcement Agencies Falls Short of Presidential Commitment Highlights Need for Federal Legislation," civilrights.org, June 23, 2003, http://www.civilrights.org/issues/cj/details.cfm?id=14156.
17. "Ashcroft Calls Patriot Act 'Key Weapon' in Fighting Terrorism," usinfo.state.gov, October 9, 2003, http://usinfo.state.gov/dhr/Archive_Index/key_weapon.html
18. Ibid.
19. Ibid.
20. Benjamin Duncan, "Fears over USA Patriot Act," english.aljazeera.net, December 15, 2003, http://english.aljazeera.net/NR/exeres/32141A53-5C17-4CE7-8B5C-76B92CID95FD.htm.
21. Ibid.
22. Mark Bryant, "Congress Urged to Amend Section 215," fortwayne.com, February 27, 2004, http://www.fortwayne.com/mld/newssentinel/8055765.htm.
23. Duncan, "Fears over USA Patriot Act," op. cit.

Chapter 9. Government Agencies

1. Personal Interview; date withheld for security purposes.
2. Ibid.
3. Personal Interview; date withheld for security purposes.

4. Ibid.
5. "'Broken Windows' Probation: The Next Step in Fighting Crime," manhattan-institute.org, August 1999, http://www. manhattan-institute.org/html/cr_7.htm.

Conclusion: Final Thoughts and Suggestions

1. Asa Hutchinson, "Cargo Containers: The Next Terrorist Target?," senate.gov, March 20, 2003, http://www.senate.gov/~gov_affairs/index.cfm?Fuseaction= Hearings.Testimony&HearingID=85&WitnessID=308&suppresslayouts=true.
2. Stacey Perman, "Meir Amit: More from the Interview with the Mossad Operative," business2.com, December 1, 2001, http://www.business2.com/b2/web/ articles/0,17863,514206,00.html.
3. Ibid.

INDEX

Abdel-Hafiz, Gamal, 2–3
Abdel-Rahman, Omar, 118–19
  at Brooklyn mosque, 63–64
Abu Ghraib prison, 117
Abuhaima, Manmoud, 72
Abuhalima, Mahmoud, 73
Abu Marzook, Musa Mohammed
  arrest of, 24–25
  profile/activities of, 21–26
Abu Namous, Omar, 56–57
Abu Nidal Organization, in American
  cities, 7
Abu Sayyaf Group, in American
  cities, 7
Abu Zuybaydah, al-Abidin Muhammed
  Husayn, and Jose Padilla, 40
Adams, Gerry, 22
Afghanistan
  al-Farouk training camp, 62, 71
  militant Islam, roots of, 8–9
  Mujahideen, 8–9
  Soviet invasion (1979), 8
African Americans
  conversion to Islam, 43–44
  on profiling, 122
African Voices Project, 44
Ahern, Jayson P., 158
Ahmad, Omar, 32
Al-Ahmed, Ali, 60
Airplane parts, counterfeit, 106–7

Akbar, Asan, 69
Alamoudi, Abdurahman Muhammad
  and Abu Marzook, 25
  arrest of, 28–33
  profile/activities of, 26–34, 51–52
Alwan, Sahim, 61
Al-Alwani, Taha Jabir, 51
Amal, xiv
American Airlines Flight 63, shoe
  bomb attempt, 41–42
"American Anointed" (Khalidi), 10
American-Arab Anti-Discrimination
  Committee, 134
American Civil Liberties Union
  (ACLU)
  interventions for Muslims, 15–16,
   49–50
  and Patriot Act, 134, 136
  on profiling, 123, 125–26
American Jewish Committee, 58
American Muslim Armed Forces and
  Veterans Affairs Council, 31,
   32–33, 52
American Muslim Council (AMC),
  26–27, 30, 32
American Muslim Foundation, 27–28,
  30, 32
Amit, Meir, 163–64
Anderson, Curt, 126
Anderson, Terry, 8

Anti-American statements, by Saudi imam, 66
Anti-Semitism
  and American-based mosques, 56
  in Islamic education textbooks, 58–60, 196–98
  by Saudi imam, 65–66
Arditi, Dani, 23
Al-Arian, Sami
  FBI indictment (text), 5, 19
  profile/activities of, 2–5, 12–20
  on talk shows, 16
Ashcroft, John, 14–15, 63, 67, 111, 128, 135
Ashrawi, Hanan, 11–12
Al-Ashwal, Shaker, 80
Automotive parts, counterfeit, 106–7
Awad, Amin, 64
Awad, Raed, 39
Ayyad, Niddal, 73

Barr, Bob, 134
Beheadings
  Daniel Pearl, 3
  and Islamic law, 57
  Nick Berg, 116–17
Beirut, U.S. Marine barracks bombing (1983), xiv, 8
Berg, Nick, 116–17
Bethlehem Neighbors for Peace, 37–38
Bilal, Ahmed Ibrahim, 63
Bilal, Muhammad Ibrahim, 63
Bilal Islamic Center, 69
Bill of Rights, free speech and terrorists, 4, 9–12, 17, 20
Bin Fahd, Abdul Aziz, Saudi Arabian prince, 55
Bin Laden, Abdullah, and World Assembly of Muslim Youth (WAMY), 66
Bin Laden, Osama
  al-Farouk training camp, 62
  al-Jazeera interview, 116
  and al Qaeda, 9

Bin Laden family, Harvard University endowments by, 11
Black Hawk Down, 78
Black September, 114
Border Patrol, 142
Boston, terrorist groups in, 6
Branch Davidians, 145
Bray, Mahdi, 112
Broken Bottles, 96–97, 108
Broken Windows theory, 96, 150
Brooklyn, al-Farooq Mosque, 63–64
Brooks, Anthony T., 18
Buckley, William, 8
Al-Buraik, Saad, 55–56, 65–66
Bush, George W.
  and Alamoudi, 26
  on al-Jazeera, 115
  protection of illegal Hispanics, 154
  racial-profiling guidelines, 126
  and U.S. safety, xxi

Cable networks, 114
Carmona, Richard, 105
Cassuccio, Ben, 82, 84–85
Catha edulis, khat from, 76
Cathinone, 76–77, 80, 90
  See also Khat
Center for Monitoring the Impact of Peace, 58
Center for Studies, Intelligence, and Information (DAM), 185–89
Chaplains. See Muslim chaplains
Charities, 8, 21–34
  and Abu Marzook, 21–26
  and Alamoudi, 26–34, 51–52
  fronts funding Hamas, 22–25
Charter of the Center of Studies, 5–7, 192–95
  purpose of, 5
  U.S cities, terrorists in, 6–7, 192–95
Chemical weapons, 157

Cheney, Dick, 116
Cigarettes, counterfeit, 98, 101–2
Cincinnati, terrorist groups in, 7
Cisneros, Henry G., 108
Clinton, Bill
    and Abu Marzook, 22–24
    and Alamoudi, 26–27, 31
Clinton, Hillary, 31
Coalition of Progressive Student
    Organizations, 17
Cohen, Stanley, 25
Cole bombing, and Kahalid "Shaikh"
    Mohammed, 3
Coloring the News (McGowan), 70
Colson, Chuck, 37
Columbia University, Islam-based
    endowments to, 10–11
Concordia University, 11
Conversion to Islam
    and African Americans, 43–44
    in prisons, 43–45
    profile of convert, 42
Council on American-Islamic
    Relations (CAIR), 24, 32, 53
Council of Islamic Schools in North
    America (CISNA), 60
Counterfeit operations, 95–108
    automobile/airplane
        parts, 106–7
    cigarettes, 98, 101–2
    confiscation, examples of, 97–98
    and intellectual-property rights
        enforcement, 107–8
    pharmaceuticals, 102–6
    positive aspects for terrorists,
        100–101
    profits from, 101
    shampoo, 97, 107
    terrorist involvement, examples
        of, 97–98
    T-shirts, 102
Counterterrorism, strategies for future,
    161–66
Crime Stoppers International, 143

Criminal offenders
    illegal aliens as, 148–51
    See also Prison system recruitment
Customs and Border Protection
    agency, 158

Dedham, Bill, 123
De Genova, Nicholas, 10
Denver, terrorist groups in, 7
Department of Homeland Security,
    140–41
    cargo container inspections, 158
    Customs and Border Protection
        agency, 158
    effectiveness of, xx, 141
    INS incorporation into, 140–41
Derwish, Kamal, 61
Designated terrorist organizations
    list of, 99–100
    U.S. actions against, 99, 110
Detroit, terrorist groups in, 7
Dirty bomb, and Jose Padilla, 40
Disinformation, examples of, 31–32
Donahue, Phil, 16
Dorda, Abuzed O., 28–29
Al-Dosari, Juma, 61–62
Drug Enforcement Agency (DEA),
    and khat-smuggling, 81, 91
Drug-smuggling
    customs seizures of, xvii
    heroin, 202–6
    by Islamic terror network, 8, 98
    opium, 98
    See also Khat
"Drugs and Terrorism: A New
    Perspective", 81
Duncan, Benjamin, 134

Edward Said Chair of Arab
    Studies, 10
Elashi, Basman, 109, 111
Elashi, Bayan, 109, 111

Elashi, Ghassan, 109–11
Elashi, Hazim, 109, 111
Elashi, Ihsan, 110–11
Elizer, Isaac, 133
Emerson, Steven, 53
Epogen, counterfeit, 102, 104
Esposito, John, 12
Ethiopia, khat grown in, 78

Al-Faisal, Saud, on Muslim
    education, 59
Fanon, Frantz, 43–44
Al-Farooq Mosque, 63–64
Al-Farouk training camp, 62
    Moussaoui description of, 71
Fasting, Ramadan, 77
Fatah, in American cities, 6–7
Fechter, Mike, 4
Federal Bureau of Investigation
    (FBI), 141–47
    Abdel-Hafiz case, 2–3
    al-Arian case, 2–4, 12–20
    overhaul after 9/11, 144–45
    problems related to, 142–44
    terrorist search after 9/11, 138
    Watch List, 141–42
Federal government
    cargo container inspection
        weaknesses, 157–59
    counterterrorism, strategies for
        future, 161–66
    infiltration by Islamic spies, 22–33,
        51–52
    intelligence agency limitations,
        138–48
    neglect of khat-smuggling, 75,
        81–82, 85–86
    neglect of mosque-terrorism link,
        72–74
    neglect of terrorism, xvii
    profiles of terrorists, lack of,
        121–22
Federal government agencies
    Department of Homeland Security,

        see Department of Homeland
        Security
    Federal Bureau of Investigation
        (FBI), see Federal Bureau of
        Investigation (FBI)
        Special Offenders Unit (SOU),
            138–40, 147
        Surveillance Unit, 137–40, 147
        unused information sources,
            147–48
    Federal-wide Drug Seizure System
        (FDSS), 79
Feinstein, Dianne, 45
Fielding, Fred F., 146
Fighel, Jonathan, 23
Finsbury Park mosque, 70–71, 113
Flight manuals, 97
Forbes, John, 96
Freeh, Louis, 25
Free speech, protection in universities,
    4, 9–12, 17, 20

Gabroni, Ali el, 72
El-Gabrowny, Ibrahim, 73
Gama'a al-Islamiyya, in American
    cities, 6–7
Ganor, Boaz, 23
Gemeaha, Mohammed, 56
Gender discrimination, in U.S. Islamic
    schools, 60
Genshaft, Judy, 17
Georgetown University, 12
Global Relief Foundation, 64
Gohara, Miriam, 127
Graduate School of Islamic and
    Social Sciences (GSISS),
        31, 44–45, 51
Gray, Patrick, 144
Great Britain
    Alamoudi arrest, 28–30
    Finsbury Park mosque, 70–71, 113
    khat-smuggling to U.S., 86–89
    Richard Reid terrorism, 41–42, 71
    terrorist groups in, 14–15

Guantanamo
  Islamic spies at, 33–34, 52
  Muslim chaplain at, 32–33

Hajj Foundation, 30
Hamas
  and Abu Marzook, 21
  in American cities, 6–7
  front for funds in U.S.,
    22–25
  funding of, 3
  and Holy Land Foundation for
    Relief and Development
    (HLF), 110–12
  and INFOCOM, 109–12
  and World Assembly of Muslim
    Youth (WAMY), 68
Hammoud, Mohamad, 98
Harris, David A., 58
Harris, Jonathan Galt, 11
Harvard University, bin Laden family
    endowments of, 11
Help the Needy, 53
Henderson, Wade, 127
Heroin-smuggler, community service
    for, 202–6
Hezbollah
  in American cities, 6–7
  Beirut bombings (1983), xiv, 8
  counterfeit goods operation, 98
  prison inmate recruitment, 49
Holy Land Foundation for Relief and
    Development (HLF),22–24,
    31–32, 39
  and Hamas, 110–12
Houston, terrorist groups in, 7
Hubbard, William K., 105
Hussein, king of Jordan, 25
Hutchinson, Asa, 159

Illegal aliens, as criminal offenders,
    148–51

Imam Muhammad Ibn Saud Islamic
    University, 55–56, 60
Imams
  in Islamic terror network, 8
  on 9/11, 55–56
  training in Saudi Arabia, 55–56
Immigration, 148–56
  Border Patrol problems, 142
  foreign students, 154
  illegal Hispanics, Bush defense
    of, 154
  illegals, as criminal offenders,
    148–51
  limiting, 152–56
Immigration and Naturalization
    Service (INS)
  and Border Patrol, 142
  limitations of, 149–50
  merge with Homeland Security,
    140–41
Indianapolis, terrorist groups in, 7
Indiana University, 62
Infant formula, counterfeit, 106
INFOCOM, 109–12
Institute for Islamic and Arabic
    Sciences, 56
Institute for Islamic and Arabic Sci-
    ences in America (IIASA), 60
Intellectual-property rights, and
    counterfeit operations, 107–8
Intelligence
  Islamic. See Islamic intelligence
  U.S. efforts. See Federal govern-
    ment agencies
International Anti-Counterfeiting
    Coalition, 107–8
International Emergency Economic
    Powers Act, 110
International Institute for Islamic
    Thought (IIIT), 14
International Policy Institute for
    Counter-Terrorism, 22–23
Internet, 112–13
  al-Jazeera on, 115

Internet *(cont.)*
drug sales, dangers of, 104–5
Islamic militant sites, 113
terrorist sites, lack of control of, 112
Intifada (1987), 13
IQRA International Education Foundation, 59
Iran
mosques, funding of, 69
roots of militant Islam, 8
Irish Republican Army (IRA), 22
prison inmate recruitment, 49
Islam
on beheading, 57
fasting on Ramadan, 77
twisted by terrorists, xviii-xix
See also Militant Islam; Wahhabism
Islamic Academy of Florida, 45
Islamic Assembly of North America
(IANA), 53
Islamic Association for Palestine (IAP),
22, 24
Islamic Center of Portland, 62–63
Islamic Circle of North America
(ICNA), 53
Islamic Committee for Palestine
(ICP), 12
Islamic Concern Project (ICP), 13, 52
Islamic Cultural Center, 56, 69
Islamic Development Bank, 30
Islamic Foundation of North America
of Queens, 59
Islamic intelligence
at Guantanamo, 33–34, 52
infiltration of U.S. government,
22–33, 51–52
Islamic schools in U.S., 57–60
anti-American/Jewish textbook
content, 58–60
gender discrimination, 60
number of, 57
Saudi Arabian funding of, 57–60, 65
and Wahhabism, 57–58, 60
Islamic Society of North America
(ISNA), 31, 44–45, 52

Islamic terror network in U.S.
and American mosques, 55–59, 61–74
in American universities, 1–20
charities of, 21–34
Charter of the Center of Studies,
5–7, 192–95
and counterfeit operations, 95–108
designated terrorist organizations,
99–100
groups in American cities, 6–7
hate speech by. *See* Propaganda by
terror networks
and Islamic schools, 57–60
and khat-smuggling, 75–94
long-range plan of, 4–5
mass media, use of, 109–19
prison system recruitment, 35–54
profiling of, 121–36
Specially Designated Global
Terrorists, 40
U.S. hesitancy to fight back, 9
waiting, tactic of, 4
IslamOnline.com, 27

Jacobson, David, 86
Jamal, Omar, 86
Al-Jazeera, 114–16
bin Laden interview, 116
on Patriot Act, 134–36
Jenkins, Brian, xix
Jersey City, al-Salaam Mosque, 63–64,
72–73
Jihad, militant preaching on, 65–66
Al-Jihad, Maktab, 113
Joint Special Operations University, xix
Jones, Pat, 159
Jose Padilla, and Abu Zuybaydah, 40

Kafirs (unbelievers), 98
Kahane, Meir, 145
Kariye, Sheik Mohamed Abdirahman,
62–63
Kashmir, 67

Kelling, George, 96
Kenya, khat grown in, 78
Kerry, John, 115
Khafagi, Bassem K., 53
Khalidi, Radhid, 10
Al-Khasy, Balai, 73
Khat, 75–94
    British smuggling to U.S.,
        86–89
    effects of, 77–78
    distribution of, 86–89
    negative side effects, 78
    neglect by U.S authorities, 76,
        81–82, 85–86
    other terms used for, 75–76
    prosecution difficulties, 90–91
    psychoactive ingredient, 76–77
    street cost, 77
    street names for, 76
    transport time/route, 80, 87,
        200–201
    U.S. Customs seizure of, 79–80,
        82–83
    use by African immigrants,
        77–78
Kidnappings
    Daniel Pearl, 3
    Terry Anderson, 8
    William Buckley, 8
Kools, Mark Fidel, 69
Kuntzman, Gersh, 56
Kyl, Jon, 31, 45, 52, 68

Lackawanna 6 case, 2, 61–62
Leadership Conference on Civil
    Rights, 122–24, 127
Levi, Edward, 144
Levi, Udi, 23
Lewis, Bernard, 153
Libya, funding of terrorism, 28–30
Lindh, John Walker, and Taliban, 125
Lopez, Aaron, 133
Los Angeles, terrorist groups in, 7

MacDonald, Heather, 155
McGahan, David, 87–88
McGowan, William, 70
MacLaverty, Bernard, 4
Marzook, Mausa Abu, 109–12
Marzook, Nadia Elashi, 109–12
Masjed As-Saber, 62–63
Al-Masri, Abu Hamza, 70, 113
Media and terrorism, 109–19
    INFOCOM case, 109–12
    Internet, 112–13
    9/11 coverage, 118
    relationship to trauma, 117–19
    television, 114–17
    See also Internet; Television
Mercy to Mankind, 59
Miami, terrorist groups in, 7
Middle East Forum, 12
Militant Islam
    converts to, 36, 42–45, 49
    moral equivalency principle, 11, 70
    roots of, 8–9
    in U.S. See Islamic terror network
        in U.S; Wahhabism
Al-Moayad, al Hasan, 63
Mohammed, Kahalid "Shaikh"
    arrest of, 3
    and 9/11, 2
    at North Carolina A&T, 2
    and USS Cole bombing, 3
Mola, Emilio, xiii
Monkey Desecrates a Mosque, A, 66,
    196–98
Moral equivalency principle, 11, 70
Mosques
    recruitment from, 61–62, 70–72
    and World Assembly of Muslim
        Youth (WAMY), 66–68
Mosques in U.S., 55–59, 61–74
    al-Zawahiri fund raising at, 64
    anti-Semitic statements, 56
    Brooklyn mosque, 63–64
    Jersey City mosque, 63–64
    Lackawanna 6 case, 61–62

Mosques in U.S. (*cont.*)
  in Los Angeles, 69
  number of, 68
  Portland 6 case, 62–63
  role changes over time, 68–69
  Saudi funding of, 57–59, 67–68
Mossad, 163–64
Mostafa, Mohamad, 105–6
Moussaoui, Zacarias
  on Afghan training camps, 71
  mosque of, 113
  and Richard Reid, 41
Mueller, Robert, 26–27
Al-Muhajiroun, in American cities, 6, 113
Muhammad, Sheikh Omar Baki, 113
Mujahideen
  splinter groups, 8–9
  in U.S., 9
Mullahs, at North Carolina A&T, 1–2
Muslim-American communities, manip-
  ulation by terror operations, 8
Muslim Brotherhood
  in American cities, 7
  in history of terrorism, 5
  and Islamic Circle of North
  America (ICNA), 53
Muslim chaplains
  at Guantanamo, 32–33, 52
  Office of the Inspector General
  (OIG) report on, 44–49
  in prison system, 35–38, 64
  training by terrorist network, 51–54
Muslim Public Affairs Council, 112
Muslims for a Better America, 24
Muslim Student Association, 17, 60

Nafi, Basheer Musa Mohammed, 14–15
Al-Najjar, Mazen
  arrest of, 2–3, 15–16
  deportation of, 3, 16
Narasaki, Karen K., 127
National Association of Muslim
  Chaplains, 36
National Drug Intelligence Center, 82

National Islamic Prison Foundation, 44
National Muslim Prison Foundation,
  33, 52
Netanyahu, Benjamin, 11, 25
New Orleans, terrorist groups in, 7
New York
  and khat distribution, 80, 82–83,
  87–94
  terrorist groups in, 6
9/11
  cost to terrorists, 103
  FBI terrorist search, 138
  hijacker connection to Saudi
  Arabia, 56
  imam remarks on, 55–56
  Islamic celebration of, 113
  and Kahalid "Shaikh" Mohammed, 2
  media coverage, 118
  U.S. safety after, xvi, xix–xxi
North American Islamic Trust
  (NAIT), 45
North Carolina Agricultural and
  Technical State University,
  Islamic extremists at, 1–2, 4, 15
North Texas Terrorism Task Force,
  109, 115
Nosair, Sayyid, 145
Nyang, Sulayman, 44

Ocean cargo containers, and WMDs
  smuggling, 157–59
Office of the Inspector General
  (OIG), on Muslim prison
  chaplains, 44–49
Olympic Games (1972) terrorism, 114
O'Neill, Paul, 23, 110
Opium, 98
O'Reilly, Bill, al-Arian interview, 16
Osman, Bassam, 45

Padilla, Jose
  arrest of, 40
  profile/activities of, 38–41

Pakistan, and World Assembly of
    Muslim Youth (WAMY), 67
Palestinian Islamic Jihad
    and al-Airan, 2, 18
    and al-Shallah, 14, 19
    in American cities, 7
Palestinian Liberation Organization
    (PLO), in American cities, 6–7
Pan Am Flight 103 bombing, 28
Pataki, George, 35–36
Patriot Act, 57, 128–29, 134
    al-Jazeera on, 134–36
"Patterns of Global Terrorism 2003,"
    98–99
Patton, George S., xx
Pearl, Daniel, and and Kahalid
    "Shaikh" Mohammed, 3
Pentagon attacks. See 9/11
Personius, Rodney O., 61
Pharmaceuticals, counterfeit, 102–6
    dangers of, 104–6
Philadelphia, terrorist groups in, 6
Philippines, and World Assembly of
    Muslim Youth (WAMY), 67
Pipes, Daniel, 12
Pistole, John, 37
Popular Front for the Liberation of
    Palestine (PFLP), 114
Powell, Colin, 160
Prison Fellowship Ministries,
    36–37
Prison system recruitment, 35–54
    and conversions to Islam, 43–45
    Muslim chaplain's anti-
        Americanism, 35–38, 64
    Office of the Inspector General
        investigation, 44–49
    Padilla recruitment, 38–41
    success, reasons for, 36–37, 42–44
Probation/parole, for suspected
    terrorists, xv-xvi
Procrit, counterfeit, 102–3
Profiling, 121–36
    ACLU on, 123, 125–26

lack of by enforcement agencies,
    121–27
limitations of, 131–32
and Patriot Act, 128–29, 134–36
public opinion of, 122
terrorists, behavioral indicators of, 131
Propaganda by terror network
    and al-Jazeera, 116
    in American universities, 9–11
    anti-American statements, 66
    anti-Semitics statements, 56, 58–60,
        65–66, 196–98
    and disinformation, 31–32
    Islamic education textbooks,
        58–60
    Muslim communities, manipulation
        of, 9
    protection as free speech, 9
    in U.S. prison system, 35–38,
        43–44
    and World Assembly of Muslim
        Youth (WAMY), 66–68
    See also Media
Prusser, Elizabeth, 88–89
Purdue University, 62

Qaddafi, Muammar, 29
Al-Qaeda
    and Abu Zuybaydah, 40
    in American cities, 6–7
    Lackawanna sleeper cell, 2,
        61–62
    post-9/11, 159–60
    prison inmate recruits of, 38–42
    Richard Reid as recruit, 41–42, 71
    roots of, 9
    training manual, 129–31
    U.S. mosque connection, 61–64
"Qat in America" (al-Ashwal), 80
Al-Qatami, Laila, 134
Qatat, al-Jazeera, 114–16
Quid, 77
Qureshi, Mohammad Javed, 39

Al-Rahim, Ahmed, 69–70
Raleigh, terrorist groups in, 7
Ramadan, fasting, 77
Rattigan, Wilfred, 3
Recruitment
    from mosques, 61–62, 70–72
    recruitee profile, 42
    training camp experience, 71
    See also Prison system recruitment
Reid, Richard Colvin
    mosque of, 71, 113
    profile/activities of, 41–42, 71
Religion and Life, 66
Reno, Janet, 128
Revell, Oliver, 22
Rice, Condoleezza
    on FBI and CIA, 146
    on U.S. offensive tactic, 4, 127
Riley, Jason L., 121–22
Rogan, Dan, 82
Romirowsky, Asaf, 11
Ruby Ridge, 145

Al-Saadawi, Alaa, 64–65
St. Louis, terrorist groups in, 7
Al-Salaam Mosque, 63–64, 72–73
Salah, Muhammad, 25
Salamah, Muhammad, 73
San Francisco, terrorist groups in, 7
Saudi Arabia
    anti-American statements, 66
    anti-Semitic statements, 65–66
    fund-raising for Palestinians, 65
    imam training institution, 55–56
    mosques (worldwide), funding of,
        67–69
    9/11 hijacker connection to, 56
    U.S. Islamic schools, funding of,
        57–60, 65
Saudi Economic Development
    Company, 30
Schools, Islamic. *See* Islamic schools
    in U.S.
Schumer, Charles, 44–45, 57, 67

September 11, 2001. *See* 9/11
Al-Shallah, Ramadan Abdullah, and
    Palestinian Islamic Jihad, 14, 19
Shampoo, counterfeit, 97, 107
Shaqaqi, Fathi, 18–19
Al-Sharif, Mohamed Ahmed, 29
Al-Sharq, 110
Shikaki, Fathi, 14
Shoe-bomber. *See* Reid, Richard
    Colvin
Sinn Féin, 22
Smith, Jane I., 44
Smith, Patty, 135
Somalia, khat use, 77–78
Somali immigrants, and khat-
    smuggling network, 82–85, 89
Somali Justice Advocacy Center,
    85–86
Soviet Union, invasion of Afghanistan
    (1979), 8
Special Offenders Unit (SOU),
    138–40, 147
Spies, Islamic. *See* Islamic intelligence
Stanford University, 12
Strossen, Nadine, 135–36
Sunrise School of Islamic Studies, 39
Surveillance Unit, 137–40, 147

Taarnby, Michael, 121
Talanian, Nancy, 134–35
Taliban, John Walker Lindh with, 125
Talk shows, al-Arian on, 16
Tampa Tribune, 4
Tel Aviv, suicide bombing (1996), 19
Television, 114–17
    al-Jazeera, 114–16
    al-Arian interviews, 16
    and audience trauma, 117–19
    cable networks, 114
    and Olympic Games (1972)
        terrorism, 114
*Terrorism: Awareness, Prevention,
    Response,* 131
Terrorism Analyst, role of, 137–38

Terror network in America. *See* Islamic terror network in U.S.

Tetrabal Corporation, 110

Textbooks, anti-American/Jewish content, 58–60, 196–98

Al-Thani, Sheik Hamad bin Khalifa, 114

Toothpaste, counterfeit, 107

Trabelsi, Nizar, 71

Training manual, al-Qaeda, 129–31

Trauma, media influence on, 117–19

T-shirts, counterfeit, 102

Umar, Warith-Deen, 36–38

Unabomber, 145

United States Marine barracks bombing (1983), and Hezbollah, xiv, 8

Universities, 1–20
  al-Arian case, 12–20
  free speech, protection of, 4, 9–12, 17, 20
  Islam-based endowments to, 10–11
  Islamic propaganda at, 9–11
  Islamic studies departments, 9–10
  protection of terrorists at, 4, 9–14, 17–20

University of Pennsylvania, 12

University of South Florida at Tampa, al-Arian case, 12–20

U.S. Commission on International Religious Freedom, 65

Viagra, counterfeit, 104

Villavivencio, Eddy, 32

Wahhabism
  death promoted by, 36
  imam training center, 55–56
  and Islamic schools/mosques in U.S., 57–58, 60
  prison inmate recruitment, 36, 49

Wahhaj, Siraj, 45

Waiting, and Islamic terrorism, 4

Warsame, Maryam, 78

Washington D.C., terrorist groups in, 7

Watch List, 141–42

Weapons of mass destruction
  dirty bomb plot, 40
  smuggling into U.S., 157–59

Weaver, Randy, 145

What Islam Is All About, 59

What Went Wrong? (Lewis), 153

White, Mary Jo, 45

Wilson, James Q., 96

World Assembly of Muslim Youth (WAMY), 57, 66–68, 196

World Islamic Call Society, 29–30

World and Islam Studies Enterprises (WISE), 12–15, 52

World Trade Center attacks. *See* 9/11

World Trade Center bombing (1993)
  alleged co-conspirators, 45
  convicted conspirators, 73
  FBI failure in, 145
  and Ramzi Yousef, 2

Wretched of the Earth, The (Fanon), 43–44

Wright, Robert, 2

Yassin, Sheik Ahmed, 67

Yemen
  funding of terrorism, 85
  khat grown in, 78, 85

Yemeni immigrants, and khat-smuggling network, 83, 85

York University, 12

Young, Michael, 65

Yousef, Ramzi, and World Trade Center bombing (1993), 2

Zagazig University, 14

Al-Zarqawi, Abu Musab, Nick Berg execution, 116–17

Al-Zawahiri, Ayman, fund raising at U.S. mosques, 64